Learning ABC's through Literature and Rhymes

Games, Activities, Patterns, Rhymes, and Stories to Make Learning the Alphabet Fun!

by
Becky White

illustrated by
Vanessa Countryman

Publisher
Key Education Publishing Company, LLC
Minneapolis, Minnesota

CONGRATULATIONS ON YOUR PURCHASE OF A KEY EDUCATION PRODUCT!

The editors at Key Education are former teachers who bring experience, enthusiasm, and quality to each and every product. Thousands of teachers have looked to the staff at Key Education for new and innovative resources to make their work more enjoyable and rewarding. Key Education is committed to developing and publishing educational materials that will assist teachers in building a strong and developmentally appropriate curriculum for young children.

PLAN FOR GREAT TEACHING EXPERIENCES WHEN YOU USE
EDUCATIONAL MATERIALS FROM KEY EDUCATION PUBLISHING COMPANY, LLC

CREDITS
Author: Becky White
Publisher: Sherrill B. Flora
Creative Director: Annette Hollister-Papp
Inside Illustrations: Vanessa Countryman
Editors: Dianne Folkerts, Audrey Rose,
        George C. Flora
Cover Illustration: Dan Sharp
Production: Key Education Staff

Key Education welcomes manuscripts and
product ideas from teachers.
For a copy of our submission guidelines,
please send a self-addressed,
stamped envelope to:

**Key Education Publishing Company, LLC
Acquisitions Department
9601 Newton Avenue South
Minneapolis, Minnesota 55431**

About the Author

Becky White has written more than three hundred educational books for Key Education, Instructional Fair, T.S. Denison, Carson-Dellosa, Good Apple, Shining Star, The Education Center, Learning Works, and McGraw Hill. Her Elementary Economics (six- book series for K-5) Published by McGraw Hill, received Learning Magazine's Teacher's Choice Gold Award for 2002. In 1980, Becky created a magazine called Shining Star for Good Apple Inc., and was the executive editor until 1993. Soon after, she created a senior magazine called A New Day for Gary Grimm and Associates and edited it until 2002. Becky is a former elementary and middle school teacher and a graduate of California University at Long Beach. Becky Daniel-White is the author of, Double Luck: Memoirs of a Chinese Orphan, a true story of a boy's struggle to escape communist China and get to America. Double Luck was published by Holiday House in 2001 and won a Parents' Choice Gold Award for nonfiction.

Some of the rhyme activities were previously published in the out-of-print title, *Mother Goose and Friends: An Alphabet Activity Book,* written by Becky White.

Introduction

Learning ABC's through Literature and Rhymes is designed to help young children build a foundation for early literacy. The activities encourage children to be active learners as they see, hear, speak, and write the basic sounds (phonemes). Activities for over 40 children's literature selections and a wealth of delightful rhymes and songs serve as the springboard for the alphabet activities.

Young children will become eager learners as they learn to name and identify upper- and lowercase letters; create projects that help them remember letter names and how to write alphabet letters; sing songs that include letter sounds; play alphabet games; listen to stories and rhymes that include specific sounds; and decorate their classrooms with bulletin boards that display alphabet letters.

Learning ABC's through Literature and Rhymes has a wealth of activities, ideas, and patterns that will keep your children interested and involved in learning all year long!

Contents

Contents

Contents

Contents

"A" Is for a Story of ABC's

CHILDREN'S BOOK:
The Book of Shadow Boxes: A Story of the ABC's
Written and illustrated by
Laura L. Seeley

This is a guided tour through the alphabet. For each letter there is a shadow box overflowing with appropriate objects. The rhymes and the hidden picture puzzles make this book a favorite choice for story time. Read the book aloud even though the children may not yet know the entire alphabet.

Seeing the letters, hearing their sounds, and associating them with pictures is a good introduction to phonemic awareness. As you read the lines, have the children take turns pointing to the appropriate objects.

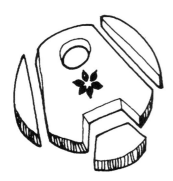

PHONICS: Letter Recognition

Directions: Slice off the bottom and top of each apple and discard those pieces. Cut the remaining portion of the apple into three or four horizontal slices. Show the children the star in the center of each slice and have them count the seeds. On waxed paper, using a plastic serrated knife, have each child carve an apple ring into the letter A. (The star in the center becomes the crossbar.) First, eat the extra pieces and then enjoy the appetizing apple-letter shape.

SHADOW BOX BOOK

Directions: Reproduce one copy of the Shadow Box pattern on page 8. Write the uppercase and lowercase A in the upper left-hand box. Then make one copy of the page for each child. The children will draw and color plus cut and paste magazine pictures of objects that begin with the letter A to complete each section on the page. (See examples below.) When finished, have them print their names on the backsides of their papers and then file each child's page separately.

As each letter of the alphabet is introduced, the children should complete the appropriate Shadow Box page. Eventually, all of the children will have 26 pages that they can collate into their very own alphabet book. Look for the Shadow Box Picture-Word Suggestions in each letter unit.

SHADOW BOX BOOK: Aa Page   (See directions above.)
Picture-Word Suggestions—acorn, apple, apricot, avocado, alligator, ants, ape, apron, angel, anchor

---

Apple Pie Begins with "A"

> **RHYME: Apple Begins with "A"**
> Apple pie, apple pudding,
> and apple pancake,
> All begin with "A."

Directions: Recite the rhyme. Show the picture card for letter A, found on page 7 in the upper right-hand corner, as the children say the rhyme. Then play the game to introduce the children to other letters of the alphabet. One at a time, show children the picture card found on the letter introduction page of each unit. (You may wish to reproduce the picture cards onto card stock and then color and cut out the cards for easier handling.) Difficult letters of the alphabet such as "X" and "U" have pictures that may need to be explained. As the leader holds up a picture card, the children substitute the name of the picture and the letter as they say new verses for the rhyme. Example: If the Bb card is held up, children would say, "Banana pie, banana pudding, and baseball bat, all begin with 'B.'" Use as many or as few cards to introduce new sounds as your group is ready to learn in one lesson. Play the game for short periods of time over an extended number of days.

Alternative: Provide the children with their own set of picture cards to color and to use as flash cards or to turn into ABC booklets.

> **RHYME: Here's ABC**
> Here's A, B, C, D, E, F, and G
> and H, I, J, K, L, M, N, O, P,
> Q, R, S, T, U, V, W, X, Y, and Z.
> And here's the child's dad,
> Who is wise and discerning,
> And knows this is the fount of learning.

Sculpting "A" Snacks

RHYME: Apple Begins with "A"
Apple pie, apple pudding
and apple pancake,
All begin with "A."

Directions: To make tasty A-shaped cookies, use thawed cookie dough. Give each child a small handful of dough to roll into a rope, using it to form an uppercase and a lowercase A. Place the letters on an aluminum foil-lined baking sheet. For children who cannot make the letter shapes, draw the shapes on the aluminum foil and let them place their dough on top of the outlines. Before putting the cookies in the oven, have the children write their initials with a pencil on the aluminum foil for easy cookie sorting later.

Thawed bread dough can be used to make individual rolls that each child can mark with an uppercase or lowercase letter before baking.

A slice of bread can be decorated by drawing the uppercase or lowercase A with apple jelly or apple butter. For easy writing, place jelly or apple butter in a squeeze bottle. You can also use the cheese that comes in cans to draw or write alphabet letters on crackers.

Remember, if children can smell cookies or bread baking and then taste the delicious flavor, they are more likely to enjoy the learning and remember the lesson!

"A's" in the Cupboard

Name _____

Directions: The cat's in the cupboard and can't see me. Can you see the cat?

Say the name of each thing you see. Circle those things that begin with the letter A. Try to find the ant, apple, acorn, alligator, apron, anchor, angel, airplane, and ape.

Animal Cut-Aparts for "A"

Directions: Reproduce this page. Cut out the animal boxes along the solid lines and staple together to make a book. Cut along the dotted lines and fold slightly on the left margin so each of the sections of each page can be viewed with other sections of other pages.

Appetizing Apples

RHYME: Apple Begins with "A"
Apple pie, apple pudding,
and apple pancake,
All begin with "A."

Apples are great for teaching the letter A. Crunch, munch, and chew any of the apple recipes below. Aaaaah, delicious! Each child will need an apple for each appetizing apple recipe. Let each child prepare his apple for the recipes that follow. Begin by washing and peeling the apple. Plastic serrated knives are sharp enough to peel and cut, yet safe enough for little hands. On a cutting board, cut the apple into halves and then quarters. Core each quarter. Cut each quarter into four equal slices. (This is a good time to introduce the concept of fractions one-half and one-quarter.)

Dried Apples

1. In a small bowl, put juice of half a lemon. Add $1/2$ c. (120 mL) water. Stir. Soak prepared apples (see preparing apple directions above) in lemon water for 2-3 minutes.
2. Thread a needle with a piece of heavy thread approximately 2 ft. (0.61 m) long. Pull thread halfway through eye of needle and knot the ends to make a 12 in. (30 cm) piece of double thread. Re-tie the knot several times so the apple slices will not slide off the end of the thread.
3. Cut a drinking straw into 15 tiny pieces. Remove apple slices from the lemon water and place them on paper towels to drain. Alternate apple pieces and straw pieces on the thread until all the apple slices are strung. Remove the needle from thread and tie a loop at top of thread. Mark each child's string of apples with his initials. Hang the strings of apples in a warm place to dry for 3–5 days.

Applesauce

Wash and peel 8–10 apples. Coarsely chop them. Place the apples, the juice from one lemon, and one thin strip of lemon rind in a slow cooker. Add 4 tbsp. (60 mL) sugar and $1/4$ c. (60 mL) water. Cover and cook the sauce on high for about 1 hour until the apples are a pulp. Rub the apples through a sieve. Add 1 tbsp. (15 mL) butter. Beat well. Cool and chill the sauce. To make apple butter, cook the apples until they are as thick as jam. Cool and chill.

"B"
Is for Beautiful Bananas and the Butter Battle Book

Bb

banana

CHILDREN'S BOOK: Beautiful Bananas
Written by Elizabeth Laird and illustrated by Liz Pichon

Beatrice sets off through the jungle to bring a beautiful bunch of bananas to her granddad. The plot thickens when curious jungle animals enter the picture. *Beautiful Bananas* offers many opportunities for children to guess what will happen next.

As you read *Beautiful Bananas,* hold up each picture and then stop and ask, "What do you think will happen next?" *(Clues in the pictures give the answers.)* To reinforce listening for details, follow up with comprehension questions.

Examples:
- What happened to the bananas?
- What happened to the flowers?

GAME: Beautiful Bananas

Beautiful Bananas has vibrant and interesting colors. After sharing the book and pictures, play a colors guessing game. After each question and child responses, show the appropriate picture.
- What color is the elephant? *(purple)*
- What color are the flowers? *(red)*
- What color is Beatrice's dress? *(pink)*
- What color are Beatrice's shoes? *(none—barefoot)*
- Which kind of animal is orange and brown? *(giraffe)*
- Name something in the story that is blue. Name something that is green.

DRAMATIZATION: Act Out the Story

Reread the story. This time as you are reading, assign parts to the children. Discuss what each character said and did.

Example: "On the way, she meets a giraffe, who flicks his tufty tail." Ask, "Who wants to be the giraffe? What does the giraffe do? What does the giraffe say?" Characters include Mother, Beatrice, giraffe, bees, monkeys, lion, parrot, elephant, and Granddad.

Directions: Act as narrator by reading story parts to connect the appearance of characters. If the children enjoy dramatization, break into smaller groups and let each group elaborate on actions and dialogue. Rehearse the skits. In a large group, take turns performing dramatizations.

GAME: Can You Eat It?

Name things that begin with "B." Children may indicate "B" foods by opening mouths wide and by closing lips tightly when it is not a "B" food..

- banana
- bread
- blanket
- birthday cake
- boat
- brass
- bell
- bead
- beets
- blueberry
- box
- berry
- beef
- book
- bug
- balloon
- broccoli
- bed
- bus
- burger
- bacon
- beans
- bridge
- bowl

LARGE GROUP ACTIVITY: Listening for Details

For this activity, each child needs three crayons—blue, black, and brown—and a large sheet of drawing paper. To reinforce listening for details, give directions and have the children draw appropriately.

- First draw a blue bunny.
- Draw a brown beetle.
- Draw a black beaver.
- Bear sees blackberries.
- Beaver sees bananas.

CHILDREN'S BOOK: The Butter Battle Book
Written and illustrated by Dr. Seuss

This book makes the /b/ sound unforgettable. Dr. Seuss wrote and illustrated over 50 children's books. A few of his titles include:

- *Bartholomew and the Oobleck*
- *Daisy-Head Mayzie*
- *Hunches in Bunches*
- *If I Ran the Circus*
- *On Beyond Zebras*
- *The Cat in a Hat*
- *The 500 Hats of Bartholomew Cubbins*
- *McElligot's Pool*
- *If I Ran the Zoo*
- *Horton Hatches the Egg*

Each of these books offer whimsical ways to teach and reinforce letters of the alphabet.

CIRCLE TIME: The Butter Battle Book

As you read *The Butter Battle Book,* ask children to listen for words beginning with /b/. Each time they hear a word beginning with the /b/ sound, they are to buzz like a bee.

CRAFT: Letter "B" Animals

Help each child draw a large uppercase and lowercase B on drawing paper. Ask the children to name animals that begin with the /b/ sound. List the names on the board. Go over the list so the children can decide which ones they would like to draw. Then have them turn the letters into those animals.

Examples:

- beetle
- bass
- bison
- bunny
- barracuda
- bird
- bug
- bat
- butterfly
- bear
- beagle
- blue jay
- baboon
- bee
- bulldog
- badger
- bighorn
- buzzard

SHADOW BOX BOOK: Bb Page
(See directions on page 7.)

Picture-Word Suggestions—balloon, banana, bear, beetle, book, button, baseball, basket, bubbles, butterfly, boot, bus, bug

---

Bowwow-Wow

RHYME: Bowwow-wow
Bowwow-wow,
Whose dog art thou?
Little Tommy Tucker's dog,
Bowwow-wow.

Directions: Use the rhyme above to play a getting-acquainted game with the children. Many children do not know each other's middle name. After the children are familiar with the rhyme, everyone repeats the first two lines of the rhyme. Then the teacher points to a child. That child says the possessive form of her full name followed by the word *dog* and the last line of the rhyme. Example: John Robert Smith's dog, bowwow-wow. Give each child a turn to say his full name. *(If a child prefers not to use her full name, allow nicknames.)*

"Bowwow," says the dog;
"Mew, mew," says the cat;
"Grunt, grunt," goes the hog;
And "squeak" goes the rat.

"Tu-whu," says the owl;
"Caw, caw," says the crow;
"Quack, quack," says the duck;
and what sparrows say you know.

Alternative: Play a guessing game with the rhyme above. When the children are seated comfortably in a circle, recite the rhyme and talk about it. The first child chooses a new animal and makes its sound. The child on his right replies, "Says the (name of that animal)." Example: First child says, "Honk, honk." The next child replies, "Says the goose." Then the second child makes a different animal sound, and the person on her right has to respond with the name of that animal. Repeat, going around the circle until everyone has had a turn.

Baa, Baa, Black Sheep

RHYME:
Baa, Baa, Black Sheep,
Baa, baa, black sheep,
Have you any wool?
Yes, sir, yes, sir,
Three bags full:
One for my master,
One for the dame,
And one for the little boy
Who lives down the lane.

Directions: Learn the rhyme and then provide each child with the outline of a sheep drawn on card stock. Using diluted white glue, have the children paint the glue on the inside of the outlines and then add cotton.

Name _____

Birds of a Feather

RHYME: Birds of a Feather
Birds of a feather flock together,
And so will pigs and swine;
Rats and mice will have their choice,
And so will I have mine.

Directions:
Color the matching birds with the same color.

Basket of "B" Foods

Name _____

Directions: Color and cut out some of your favorite foods (page 19) that begin with the letter B. Paste them in the basket below. Color the basket your favorite color. Make it beautiful!

Basket of "B" Food Patterns

Learning ABC's Through Literature and Rhymes

"C" Is for Curious Kids and Carl

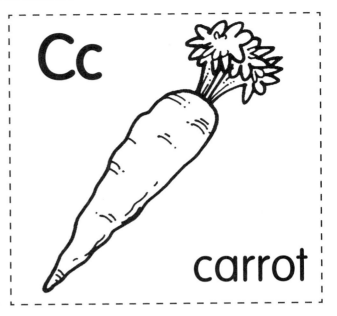

CHILDREN'S BOOK: The Big Book of Words for Curious Kids
Created by Heloise Antoine and illustrated by Ingrid Godon

This collection of hundreds of words that kids can identify with is what might be called a "pictionary." Each word is printed beneath a picture so children can make quick associations. Content topics include clothing, playtime, shopping, kitchen, eating, preschool, garden, pets and animals, grown-up things, bathroom, and bedroom. The pictures are a bit small for sharing in a large group, so they are best used in small group situations.

Introduce the book by showing the pictures and reading the topics—not each word. Let the children take turns guessing the words printed below the pictures. Explain that you will place the book in a learning center where children will be using it to complete games and activities.

LEARNING CENTER: Curious Kids

Place *The Big Book of Words for Curious Kids* in a learning center where children can "read" it. Include other big books of words by the same author: *Curious Kids Go to Preschool and Curious Kids Go on Vacation. (See activity ideas below.)*

PHONICS: Letter Recognition

Everyday pass out a blank index card to each child. Ask the children to find a word beginning with a particular letter, print it on one side of the card, and then illustrate the word on the backside. Use a paper punch to put a hole in each word card. Encourage the children to keep their special word cards on a large metal ring. Allow time for pairs of children to share their words and pictures with each other.

GAME: Hide-and-Seek Words

Play a hide-and-seek game with words and pictures. Each day, bring in an object that can be found in the big word book(s). Place it in the learning center. Challenge the children to find a picture of the object in the book(s). In this process, the children will learn that the words are organized by topics. For example, if it is a comb, its picture can be found on the bathroom page.

GAME: It's the Same

Another fine game to play using these word books is called "It's the Same." Read a word and point to a picture on the edge of the page. The children must then find the same object in the center of the page and name it.

CHILDREN'S BOOKS:
Curious Kids Go to Preschool and Curious Kids Go on Vacation
Written by Heloise Antoine and illustrated by Ingrid Godon

These books have additional common words organized by topics. *Curious Kids Go to Preschool* includes the following: first day, playtime, art class, gym class, in the rest room, time to eat, time to rest, on the playground, teachers, special occasions, and class photo. Topics included in *Curious Kids Go on Vacation*: packing, on the road, the country, the train, the beach, the ferry, camping, the mountains, rainy day, and the airport.

Share these books with small groups of children. After you show a page and read the topic, say, "Can you point to a picture of a word beginning with /c/? With /b/? With /a/?"

PHONICS: Letter Recognition

Pass out large cards with a letter "A," "B," or "C" on each. Read words from the books. When the children hear a word that begins with the sound of the letter on their card, they hold up the letter card.

GAME: Guess the Picture

This game can be used with many different picture books, but the big word books lend themselves extremely well to this kind of play. Open a book. Give clues about an object in the pictures. The children use the clues to find the matching picture. Examples: Ball—It begins with "B." It's blue with yellow spots. It's in a corner of a page.

CHILDREN'S BOOK: Good Dog, Carl
Written and illustrated by Alexandra Day

This is a wordless book that encourages a different story every time it is shared. This book and others in the "Carl" series are excellent for teaching sequence of events. As you show each page, have the children take turns describing what is happening. After sharing the book with the children, discuss what happened after or before certain events.

CRAFTS: "C" Foods

Have the children draw an all "C" breakfast, lunch, snack, or dessert. Pass out large paper plates. The children will "fill" their plates with "C" foods. List on the board the names of foods that begin with the hard /c/ sound.

Examples:

- cabbage
- cake
- candy cane
- cobbler
- carrots
- corn
- cotton candy
- caramel
- cauliflower
- coleslaw
- casserole
- cantaloupe
- cookies
- cupcake
- corn bread
- collards
- coffee cake
- candy
- calzone
- cucumber

SHADOW BOX BOOK: Cc Page
(See directions on page 7.)

Picture-Word Suggestions—cab, cat, candy, camel, caterpillar, candle, carrot, cap, cow, cookie, cup, cupcake, corn, coat, car, can

---

Come Up, Go Down

RHYME: Come Up, Go Down

Come, my dear children,
Up is the sun,
Birds are all singing,
And morn has begun.

Up from the bed, Miss,
Out on the lea;
The horses are waiting
For you and for me!

Cantaloupes!
Cantaloupes!
What is the price?
Eight for a dollar,
And all very nice.

Use this rhyme as a springboard for discussing morning events, like the sun coming up, and evening events, like the sun setting. This discussion can take a number of different directions. Here are a few examples:

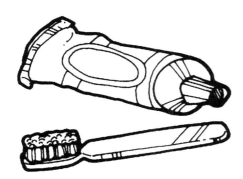

Morning and Evening Routines

Ask children to describe their morning and evening routines. Make a list. When do they get up? What do they do next? Make a graph. How many children are brushing their teeth at the same time? Talk about nature's morning and evening routines (sun rising and setting, birds singing and resting, flowers opening and closing, and so on).

Up and Down and Opposites

How many opposite pairs can your children name? Have pairs of children try to act them out. Label all of the opposites in your classroom.

Morning and Evening Mobile

Take one sheet of white paper and glue it to the same size sheet of black paper. Give each child a piece about 4 in. (10 cm) square. The children can cut their pieces into a shape if they desire. Direct the children to draw (or cut out and paste) pictures of daytime things on the white side and nighttime things on the black side. Punch a hole in the top of each child's finished work and attach a string. Hang the pieces from a coat hanger or create a more elaborate suspension system (the cardboard tubing from some coat hangers works well). Vary the lengths of the string to balance the mobile.

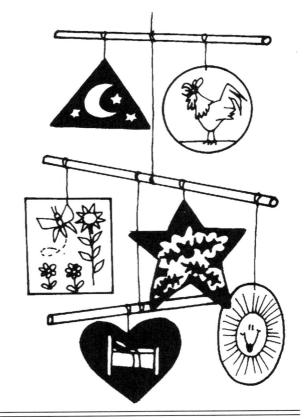

Open the Gate, Charley

RHYME:
Charley Warley Had a Cow
Charley Warley had a cow,
Black and white about the brow,
Open the gate and let her through
Charley Warley's old cow!

Directions: This game is played similar to "London Bridge." Two children form a bridge with their arms. The rest of the children line up single file behind the "bridge." Children run under the "bridge" singing the rhyme. (Use the tune of "London Bridge.") When the last word of the rhyme is said, the bridge comes down trapping one child inside. That child must say the name of an animal that begins with /c/ like "cow."

After answering, the "bridge" opens again and the game continues. The line moves again while everyone sings the new rhyme substituting the "C" animal named. Example: If one child says "camel," the children sing: "Charley Warley had a camel. Black and white about the brow. Open the gate and let her through, Charley Warley's old camel!"

Examples: cow, cat, chipmunk, clam, cheetah, chimpanzee, camel, chicken, cobra, cougar

Letter "C" Crayon Resist

Crayon resist is a technique of painting. Begin by having the children use white crayons to draw and color several letter Cs on their papers. It is important to cover the letters with a thick layer of crayon. Prepare a thin mixture of black tempera paint. Place the drawings on newspaper. Let the children lightly brush one coat of paint over their entire pictures. The letter Cs will resist the paint and show up white. Allow the paintings to dry before removing them from the newspapers.

"D"
Is for Ducks

CHILDREN'S BOOK:
The Littlest Duckling
Written by Gail Herman and
illustrated by Ann Schweninger

This book is about a busy day for a mama duck and four ducklings. *The Littlest Duckling* is excellent for teaching ordinal numbers: first, second, third, and fourth. Reinforce listening skills by having the children point to each duck as it is mentioned in the story.

Example: "I'm here," said the first little duckling. Ask, "Where is the first duckling?"

CRAFT: Ducks

Reproduce the duckling patterns (see page 25) onto red, blue, yellow, and green construction paper. Each child will have four ducks—different colors and different sizes. Not everyone's largest duck will be red, etc. Have the children line up their ducks according to your directions.

Examples:
• Put the red duck first, followed by the blue duck, green duck, and then the yellow duck.
• Line up the ducks from smallest to largest. Largest to smallest.
• What color is your largest duck? Smallest duck?
• Put the largest duck under the smallest duck.

GAME: Waddle, Waddle, Quack, Quack

As you say words, the children must decide if the words describe movements or sounds. They might indicate movements by flapping their arms like duck wings and indicate sounds by quacking.

Examples:
• squeak	• walk	• tramp	• trot	• dash	• holler	• growl	• whimper
• screech	• squeal	• shriek	• strut	• roar	• sing	• stroll	• howl

CHILDREN'S BOOK: John Philip Duck
Written and illustrated by Patricia Polacco

This story is loosely based on the famous Peabody Hotel ducks. To reinforce listening skills, ask the children to listen for all the places the hotel staff hid the duck and how the duck got it's name. Then read the book aloud. After the story has been read, discuss the story. Ask:
• Who hid the duck under a lid? (chef)
• Where did the valet keep the duck? (under his hat)
• Who hid the duck on her cart? (manicurist)
• Where did the valet keep the duck? (under his hat)
• Where did the front-desk crew keep the duck? (empty key box)

GAME: The Movement March

Play a John Philip Sousa march for the class. Keeping time, everyone waddles like ducks to the march. Have the children move like other animals to the music, too.

- gallop like horse
- tromp like elephants
- bound like a kangaroo
- strut like peacocks
- leap like a frog
- hop like a rabbit

SHADOW BOX BOOK: Dd Page
(See directions on page 7.)

Picture-Word Suggestions—dog, donkey, dinosaur, dolphin, doll, door, duck, dish, dominoes, daffodils, daisy

---

Duckling Patterns

(See directions on page 24.)

Dance, Thumbkin

RHYME: Dance Thumbkin

Dance, Thumbkin, dance;	(Tuck in fingers; wiggle thumbs.)
Dance, ye merrymen, everyone;	(Wiggle all fingers and thumbs.)
For Thumbkin he can dance alone,	(Wiggle only the thumbs.)
Thumbkin he can dance alone.	(Wiggle only the thumbs.)
Dance, Foreman, dance;	(Wiggle only index fingers.)
Dance, ye merrymen, everyone;	(Wiggle all fingers and thumbs.)
For Foreman he can dance alone,	(Wiggle only index fingers.)
Foreman he can dance alone.	(Wiggle only index fingers.)
Dance, Longman, dance;	(Wiggle only middle fingers.)
Dance, ye merrymen, everyone;	(Wiggle all fingers and thumbs.)
For Longman he can dance alone,	(Wiggle only middle fingers.)
Longman he can dance alone.	(Wiggle only middle fingers.)
Dance, Ringman, dance;	(Wiggle only ring fingers.)
Dance, ye merrymen, everyone;	(Wiggle all fingers and thumbs.)
For Ringman he can dance alone,	(Wiggle only ring fingers.)
Ringman he can dance alone.	(Wiggle only ring fingers.)
Dance, Littleman, dance;	(Wiggle only little fingers.)
Dance, ye merrymen, everyone;	(Wiggle all fingers and thumbs.)
For Littleman he can dance alone,	(Wiggle only little fingers.)
Littleman he can dance alone.	(Wiggle only little fingers.)

Use indicated hand motions to turn the rhyme into a finger play.

After children are familiar with the song and actions, draw a simple face on each of their fingers with a fine-tip, washable marker. Perform the action song again using the finger puppets.

RHYME:
Dickery, Dickery, Dock
Dickery, dickery, dock;
The mouse ran up the clock;
The clock struck one,
The mouse ran down,
Dickery, dickery, dock.

RHYME:
Deedle, Deedle, Dumpling
Deedle, deedle, dumpling, my son Jon,
Went to bed with his stockings on;
One shoe off, and one shoe on,
Deedle, deedle, dumpling, my son Jon.

"D" Picture Dominoes

Getting Ready: Copy the dominoes on pages 27–29 onto card stock and then cut them apart.

Directions: This game can be played by two to four players. Turn the dominoes facedown and spread them out. Each player selects seven dominoes and places them faceup in front of them. The cards left facedown are called the bone pile. Turn over one domino from the bone pile. This is the beginning of the zoo train. The first player must play on either end of the train by placing a matching domino from his seven. A match is two identical animals. If a player cannot make a match with the dominoes from his pile, he must continue drawing dominoes from the bone pile until he can make a match. Then the next player gets a turn. Players can add to either end of the domino zoo train. Players continue to build the zoo train by making matches until one player has used up all of her dominoes. If the bone pile is exhausted, the players simply skip turns when they cannot make a match.

"E" Is for Eating the Alphabet

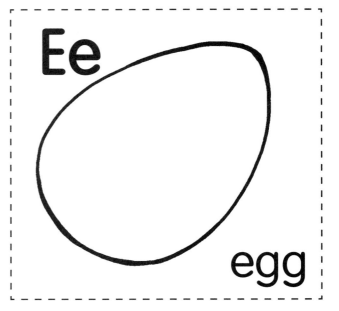

CHILDREN'S BOOK:
Eating the Alphabet: Fruits and Vegetables from A to Z
Written and illustrated by Lois Ehlert
This book contains brilliant watercolor collages. The alphabet in uppercase and lowercase letters plus fruit and vegetable words are presented. Let children "read" this book aloud. As you show each page, have the children take turns saying the words next to the pictures.

LARGE GROUP ACTIVITY: Classifying
As you present each page, ask questions.
Examples:
1. How many fruits are shown on this page? Vegetables? More fruits or vegetables?
2. What is the largest fruit? Smallest fruit? Largest vegetable? Smallest vegetable?
3. What color is the smallest vegetable? Smallest fruit? Largest vegetable?
4. Which food is the roundest? Longest?
5. How many foods are round? Not round?
6. Which food takes up the most space on the page? Least amount of space on the page?
7. Which food would you like to eat? Not want to eat?
8. Which food is the smoothest? Roughest?
9. Which ones on this page are the same color?
10. Which one is the most colorful?
11. Which ones have you tasted? Never tasted?
12. Which ones are usually eaten cold? Eaten hot?
13. Name the round, red fruit on this page. Name the squarish, green vegetable.

GAME: Play Twenty Questions
Reinforce listening for details by having one child choose a secret fruit or vegetable. The remaining children take turns asking "yes" and "no" questions. *Example:* (Eggplant is the secret food.) Ask, "Is it a vegetable?" "Is it green?"" Is it eaten raw?"

PHONICS: Letter-Sound Recognition
Use the coloring sheet on page 31 for children to practice identifying the first sounds of words.

SHADOW BOX BOOK: Ee Page   (See directions on page 7.)
Picture-Word Suggestions—egg, eggplant, elf, elk, eagle, eel, emu, eclair
---

Name _____

Let's Eat

Directions: Color the fruits and vegetables. Write the letter that makes the first sound you hear when you say the name of each food.

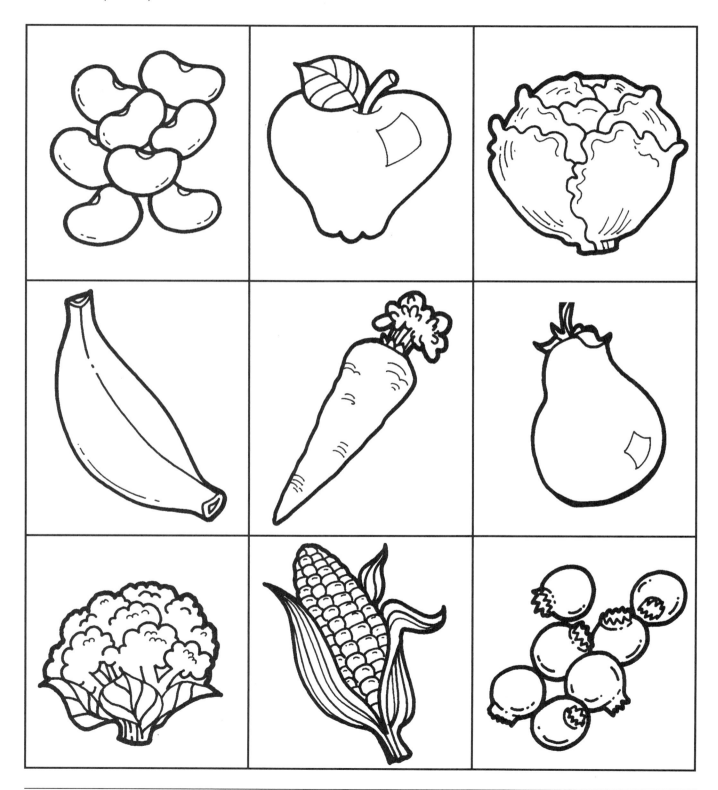

"E" Is for Echo-echooo-echooo

RHYME: Early to Bed

Early to bed and early to rise
Makes a man healthy,
Wealthy, and wise.

To practice learning all three rhymes on this page, play an echo game. The leader says a word, phrase, or line and the children echo it.

The following rhyme is good to echo by repeating each word three times:

RHYME: Eggs, Butter, Cheese

Eggs, butter, cheese, bread,
Stick, stock, stone, dead.
(Repeat each word three times.)

To learn the second rhyme, break it into phrases.

RHYME: Elsie Marley Has Grown So Fine

Elsie Marley has grown so fine,	Elsie Marley, Marley, Marley has grown so fine, fine, fine,
She won't get up to serve the swine;	She won't get up, up, up to serve the swine, swine, swine;
But lies in bed till eight or nine,	But lies in bed, bed, bed till eight or nine, nine, nine,
And surely she does take her time.	And surely she does, does, does take her time, time, time.

The third rhyme can be memorized by echoing the last word in each line.

RHYME: Early to Bed

Early to bed and early to rise   Rise, rise, rise
Makes a man healthy, wealthy, and wise.   Wise, wise, wise

E. L. Ephant

Directions: Have the children use the head and trunk patterns on page 34 and the uppercase E below to make E. L. Ephant. Color and cut out the patterns. Glue the head and trunk where indicated. Fold the trunk on the dotted lines in accordion-fashion. Use E. L. Ephant to celebrate the letter E and have an autograph party. Encourage the children to collect signatures from people who have the letter E in their names.

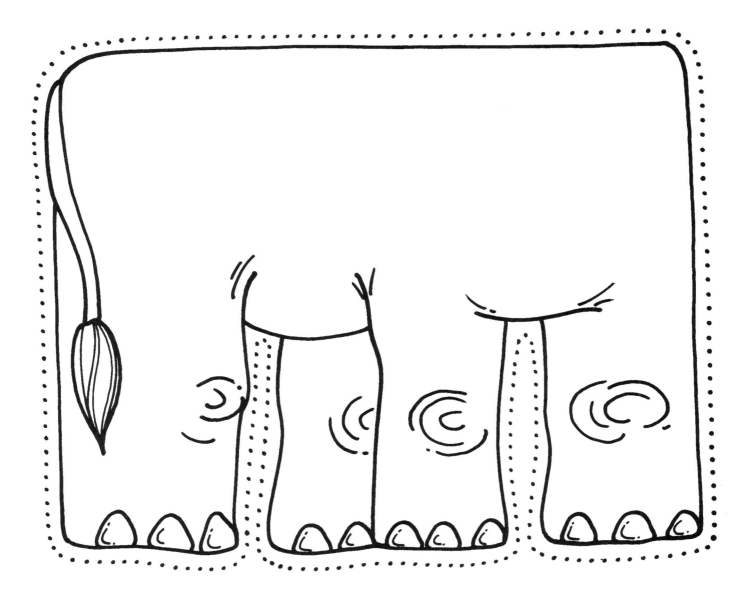

E. L. Ephant Patterns

ee

"F" Is for Franklin and Fish

Ff
fish

CHILDREN'S BOOK:
Franklin Rides a Bike
Written by Paulette Boureois and illustrated by Brenda Clark

This story will help your children realize that everybody struggles while learning something new. Franklin is a turtle with whom many children will identify. Worried that his friends will make fun of the training wheels on his bike, Franklin misses out on a lot of fun. How he gains the courage to ride without the training wheels offers a good lesson on "if at first you don't succeed, try, try again."

Read the story aloud. Follow up by discussing bicycles. Who once upon a time had training wheels on his bike? Exchange learning-to-ride bike stories.

There are dozens of Franklin books. Each centers around a problem that your children may have experienced. Share other Franklin books:

- *Franklin's New Friend*
- *Franklin Is Messy*
- *Franklin's Bad Day*
- *Franklin Fibs*
- *Franklin and the Thunderstorm*
- *Franklin Has a Sleepover*
- *Franklin's Secret Club*
- *Franklin Says "I Love You"*
- *Franklin and the Toothfairy*
- *Franklin and the Baby-sitter*

CRAFT: Fancy Me Ribbons

Getting Ready: On blue construction paper, reproduce a Fancy Me Ribbon (see page 36) for each child in your class.

Directions: Begin by discussing the things that Franklin could do well: swim underwater, hit home runs, climb the monkey bars, and pump high on the swings. Invite the children to name five things that they do well. Pass out the blue ribbons. Help the children print their accomplishments on their ribbons.

SHADOW BOX BOOK: Ff Page   (See directions on page 7.)
Picture-Word Suggestions—foot, face, fan, firefighter, fish, four, five, fox, fur, family, farm, feather, fork, fence, fern

---

Fancy Me Ribbon Pattern

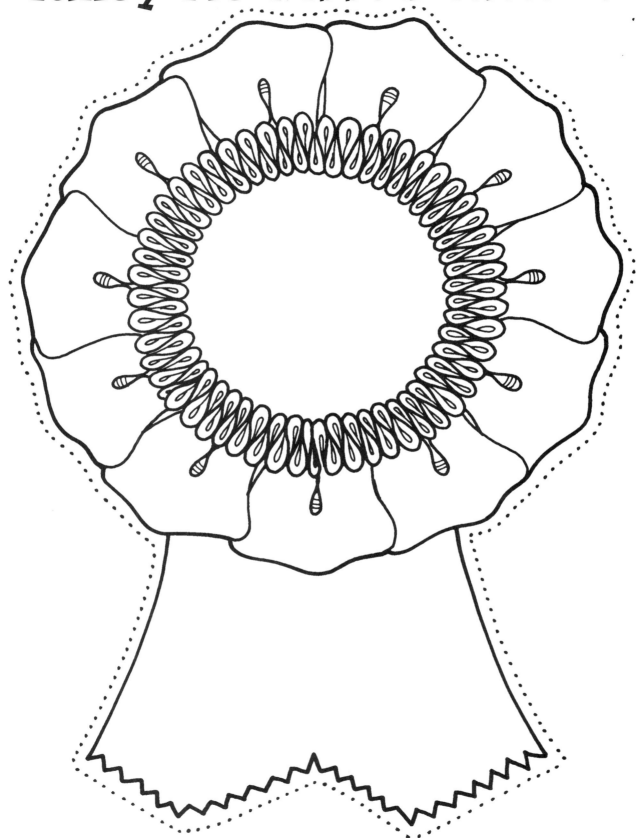

Sing a Song of Foxes

RHYME: "F" Was a Fox
"F" was a fox,
So cunning and sly,
Who looks at the hen roost.
Need I need why?

Directions: Use the tune of "Ten Little Indians" to create new songs for celebrating the letter F.

Example:
One little,
Two little,
Three little foxes.
Four little,
Five little,
Six little foxes.
Seven little,
Eight little,
Nine little foxes.
Ten little foxes here.

Alternative: To reinforce counting to 10, this rhyme can be turned into an action song (see verses above). Children are to hold up both hands with fingers down, forming two fists. The appropriate number of fingers are shown while singing each line of the song. Have the children take turns making up new songs by replacing the word "foxes" with the names of other objects, especially animals, that begin with the letter F, such as fawn, fish, firefly, and frog. After the children have invented new verses for the song, instead of counting animals that begin with F, make up verses that tell how they move. Youngsters make the appropriate movements as they sing the new songs, too.

Example:
Hop little,
Hop little,
Hop little froggies.
Hop little,
Hop little,
Hop little froggies, . . .
Hop little,
Hop little,
Hop to your lily pad, now.

Other verses:
Glow little firefly.
Leap little flea.
Swim little fish.
Run little fawn.
Fly little fly.

Fingerprint "F" Things

Discuss fingerprints. Explain that everyone has different fingerprints. Have children use a stamp pad (water-soluble ink) to make their own fingerprints on white construction paper. Provide soapy water and towels for cleanup. By adding details with fine-tip washable markers, the children can turn each fingerprint into an object that begins with the letter F in its name. Share the list below to help the children get started.

Examples:

fox	fan	fern	feather
flag	flake	fruit	fly
fawn	fish	flea	firefly
frog	fig	face	feet
fire	foot	flower	

Funny Faces

RHYME: Funny Face

Little Tommy Grace had a pain in his face,
So bad he could not learn a letter;
When in came Dicky Long,
Singing such a funny song,
That Tommy laughed,
And found his face much better.

Getting Ready: Your children will have fun playing this funny faces game. Here is what you'll need, a spinner dial, a paper plate for each player, and the picture collection of eyes, eyebrows, noses, mouths, and ears (either cut from magazines, drawn by the children, or copies of page 39).

Copy the patterns below onto card stock. Cut them out and attach the arrow with a paper fastener.

Directions: Have the children determine who will start the game. Players spin to see which face part they will choose. They make a selection and place it on the appropriate place on their paper plate "face." If a player spins but has already selected that face part, the child cannot play and passes the dial to the next player. The first player to complete a "funny face" is the winner.

Alternative: This game works best with human features; however, if the children are ready for a challenge, have them create animal faces.

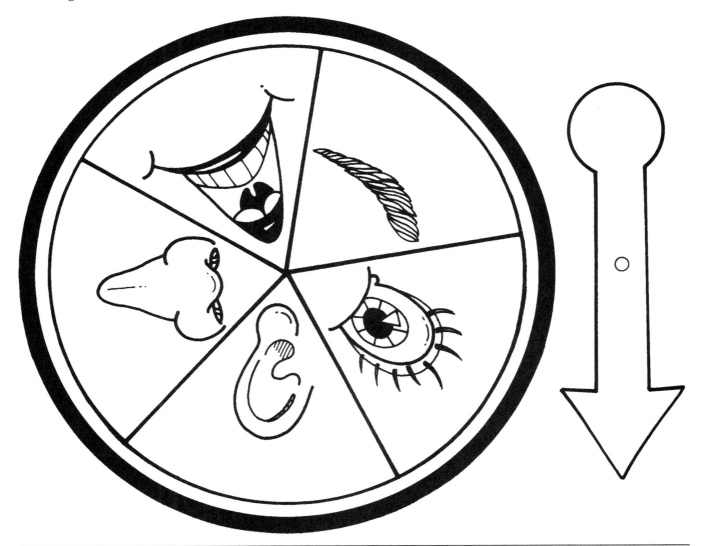

Funny Face Patterns

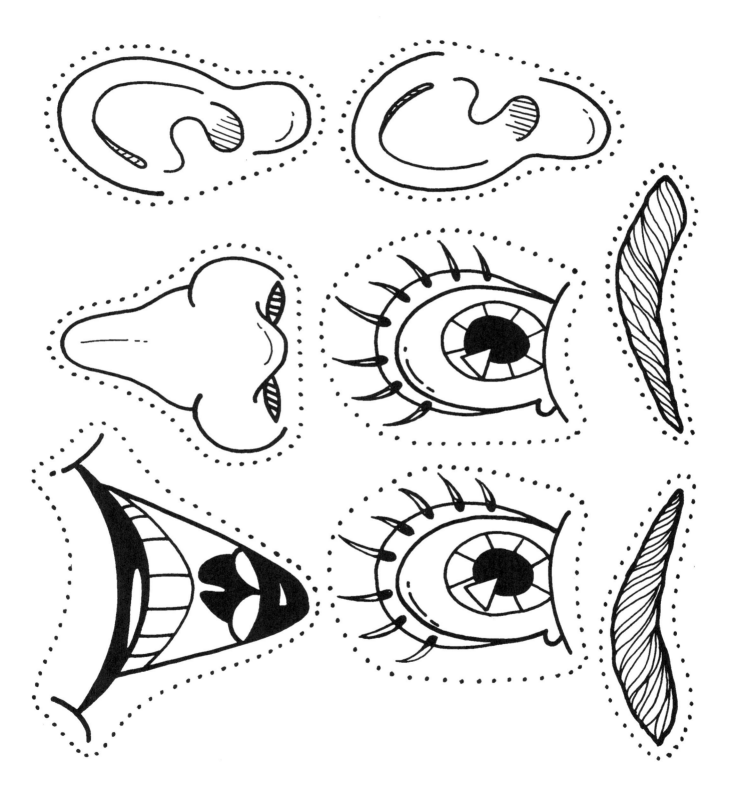

"G"
Is for George

CHILDREN'S BOOK:
Curious George Learns the Alphabet
Written and illustrated by H. A. Rey

The Complete Adventures of Curious George contains *Curious George Learns the Alphabet,* plus these six other Curious George stories:

- *Curious George*
- *Curious George Takes a Job*
- *Curious George Rides a Bike*
- *Curious George Gets a Medal*
- *Curious George Flies a Kite*
- *Curious George Goes to the Hospital*

George is a monkey that lives with his friend who wears a yellow hat. The author describes George as "a good little monkey and always very curious." Read aloud the story *Curious George Learns the Alphabet.* When George looks at some books, he is curious. What are all those little black marks and dots and lines? His friend in the yellow hat tells George that stories are made of words and words are made of letters.

PHONEMIC AWARENESS: Soft /G/ Words

Say the /j/ sound that begins the word "George." Ask the children to think of other words that begin like that sound. Make a list on the board. Give clues for soft /g/ words while children guess.

Examples:
- a house-shaped cake decorated with candy (gingerbread house)
- a large room where people can play basketball (gym)
- an animal with a very long neck (giraffe)
- a hamster-like animal (gerbil)
- a certain kind of dog (German shepherd)
- a southern American state (Georgia)

PHONICS: Letter Recognition

Give each child a paper bag. Have the children write the large letters A–G on the front of their bags. The children will take home the bags, find one thing that begins with each of the seven letters, and put the objects in their bags. Back in class, have the children take turns removing their seven items, one at a time, as others take turns naming each object and identifying the correct beginning letter.

CHILDREN'S BOOK: It's George!
Written by Miriam Cohen and illustrated by Lillian Hoban

This story is about George, who could not spell, but could do other things well. Before sharing the book, ask the children if they think being smart is something that comes with practice. Tell them to listen and decide if Anna Maria is as smart as she thinks. Follow up with a discussion.

- Do you know someone named George?
- How did George save a life?
- Name one of the gentle things that George did.

Other titles about this multi-ethnic classroom with a loving teacher are as follows:

- *Will I Have a Friend?*
- *Best Friends*
- *The New Teacher*
- *Tough Jim*
- *When Will I Read?*
- *"Bee" My Valentine!*
- *Liar, Liar, Pants on Fire!*
- *Starting First Grade*
- *Jim's Dog Muffins*
- *See You Tomorrow, Charles*
- *No Good in Art*
- *Lost in the Museum*

GAME: Guess the Sound

Explain that the letter G does not always make a soft /j/ sound like in "George." Sometimes the letter G makes a hard sound as in the word "gum." Teach the children the sign language for the letters G and J.

G   **J**

As you say G words, have the children indicate whether they hear the hard or soft /g/ sound by motioning with sign language.

Examples:
- girl
- gorilla
- ghost
- goat
- giraffe
- gerbil
- garden
- gum
- guitar
- gift
- guppies
- gazelle
- goose
- giant
- gull
- gingerbread
- gate
- gentle

SHADOW BOX BOOK: Gg Page   (See directions on page 7.)
Picture-Word Suggestions—girl, goat, garden, gift, goose, gorilla, gum, gumball, guppy, ghost, guitar, gate, gull

---

Good People Give Ear

Directions: The human body is the most extraordinary musical instrument of all! It can make an infinite number of sounds. Explore some of these sounds with your class. Challenge the children to see how many different sounds they can make with their bodies, such as click their tongues, drum their faces, slap their hips, stomp their feet, and whistle, hum, clap, and snap their fingers.

RHYME: Good People Give Ear
Good people all, of every sort,
Give ear unto my song:
And if you find it wondrous short,
It cannot hold you long.

List the sounds on the board. Practice the different sounds so that the children can try them all! Assign a sound to each child or small group. As one child or small group recites a "G" rhyme, the others keep time with sounds they make with their bodies. As you lead the human orchestra, raise your hand for the sound to be louder and also lower your hand to quiet the sounds. How harmonic can the class become?

Good Horses, Bad Horses

RHYME: Good Horses, Bad Horses
Good horses, bad horses,
What is the time of day?
Three o'clock, four o'clock,
Now fare you away.

RHYME: Georgey Porgey
Georgey Porgey, pudding and pie,
Kissed the girls and made them cry;
When the girls came out to play,
Georgey Porgey ran away.

Directions: "Good Horses, Bad Horses" is an out-of-doors tag game. Divide the class in half. One half of the children are "horses," the other half are "trees." Place the "trees" about 6 ft. (1.8 m) from each other so that there is space to run between them. As the "trees" stand grounded in a spot, the "horses" chant the rhyme and run in between and around them. The "trees" reach out with their branches (arms) and try to tag the "horses" that run by. If a "horse" is tagged, he becomes a "tree" and must stay in place. After a while the teacher blows a whistle and everyone freezes. When she blows the whistle a second time, the "trees" become "horses," and the "horses" become "trees." The game continues as the "horses" chant and run in between the new "trees." Play until children tire of the game.

Variation: The rhyme can also be used to begin a race. The two runners chant the rhyme and when they say the last word "away," the race is on!

Directions: Use the rhyme "Georgey Porgey" to play a tag game, too. Choose three children to be Georgey Porgey and one child to be the fairy who carries a drinking-straw wand. As the other children run around, the Georgey Porgeys try to tag players. If a child is tagged, he is grounded and makes a crying sound to let the fairy know that he has been caught. When the fairy taps the child with the magic wand (drinking straw), he is free to again.

Goose, Goat, and Gorilla

RHYME:
Goosey, Goosey, Gander
Goosey, goosey, gander,
Wither dost thou wander?
Upstairs, and downstairs, and
In my lady's chamber.

Directions: Discuss the sound of the letter G as in goosey. Have the children recite the rhyme. Then make a stuffed felt goose or another "G" animal. Each child will need a pattern (on page 44), felt, cotton balls or tissue for stuffing, needle and thread, yarn scraps, pencil, washable markers, and scissors. Let the children choose a color of felt they like. Be sure there is enough felt for two goose-shaped pieces.

1. Place the pattern on top of the felt and use a pencil to trace around the outline.

2. Repeat this step again because the goose needs two sides.

3. Use a black marker to draw an eye on both pieces. Cut out on the outline.

4. Allow each child to sew along the bottom edge as shown in the diagram. Stuff the opening of the animal with cotton balls or stuffing.

5. Put a yarn loop on each animal to serve as a hanger.

6. Have an adult or older child sew around the rest of the animal to close its body.

Goose Pattern

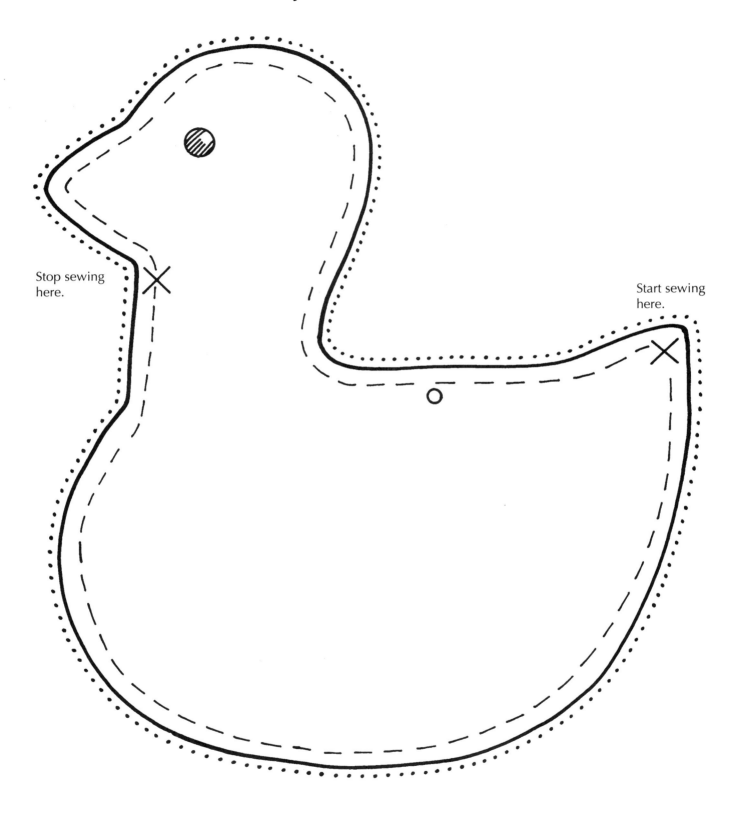

Stop sewing here.

Start sewing here.

"H"
Is for a Story of ABC's

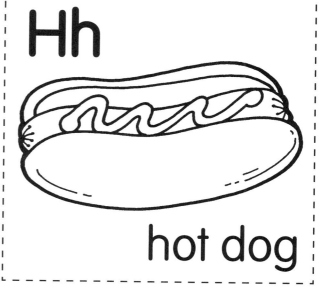

Hh

hot dog

CHILDREN'S BOOK:
Harold and the Purple Crayon
Written by Crockett Johnson

This wordless book will delight children as much today as it did when it was first published 50 years ago. As you turn the pages, encourage the children to take turns describing what is happening. Follow up by having the children use a purple crayon to draw a picture of "H" animals.

Write the list on the board and review it as many times as needed until the children have decided which "H" animals they will draw. Help the children write the names of their animals under their pictures.

Examples:

- hen
- hyena
- hare
- hippo
- hog
- hedgehog
- hawk
- honeybee
- hermit crab
- horned toad
- horse
- hummingbird
- hammerhead shark
- heron

CHILDREN'S BOOK: Hop on Pop
Written and illustrated by Dr. Seuss

Uncomplicated, monosyllabic rhymes are used to foster learning and inspire children to read. Other "I Can Read It All by Myself Beginner Books" by Dr. Seuss are listed as follows:

- *Green Eggs and Ham*
- *One Fish Two Fish Red Fish Blue Fish*
- *Fox in Socks*
- *Oh the Things You Can Think*

CIRCLE TIME: Rhyming Words

Read aloud *Hop on Pop* without pausing for discussion. Then reread the book, having the children listen for rhyming words. Pausing after each page for child input, make a list of rhyming words on the board, such as "hop" and "Pop." Write the letter b in front of -op. Say, "Can anyone read the new word?" Ask the children what the word "bop" would be if the beginning sound was changed to /c/, /m/ or /t/. When new rhyming words have been created, use them to make sentences. Example: Mop the top of Pop. In the same fashion, continue with other rhymes from the book. Create lists of rhyming words and use them in sentences. Follow up by making Rhyming Word Wheels (see page 46). Have the children make these words: bat, bed, bop, cat, cop, cup, fat, fed, hat, hop, mat, mop, pat, pop, pup, rat, red, sat, sop, sup, Ted, top, wed.

GAME: Hopscotch

Give children an opportunity to practice hopping by playing various hopscotch games. Draw a hopscotch pattern on a sidewalk or asphalt surface, or use masking tape to designate the playing area inside the classroom. Instead of numerals, randomly place letters A–J in the squares.

Directions: Use the hopscotch area to practice standing on one foot and hopping. Give directions to be followed by a player. For example: Say, "Hop to the letter A and back again. Hop to the letter B and stop." The children may also play games requiring them to hop with two feet together, walking backwards, or hopping on tiptoes.

SHADOW BOX BOOK: Hh Page   (See directions on page 7.)
Picture-Word Suggestions—hair, hat, hay, head, heart, hen, hippo, hog, hyena, horse, harp, horn

---

Rhyming Word Wheel Patterns

Directions: Reproduce the patterns below onto card stock. Cut out the wheels. Center the small wheel on top of the large wheel. Attach the centers with a paper fastener so that the wheels move freely. Turn the small wheel to make words.

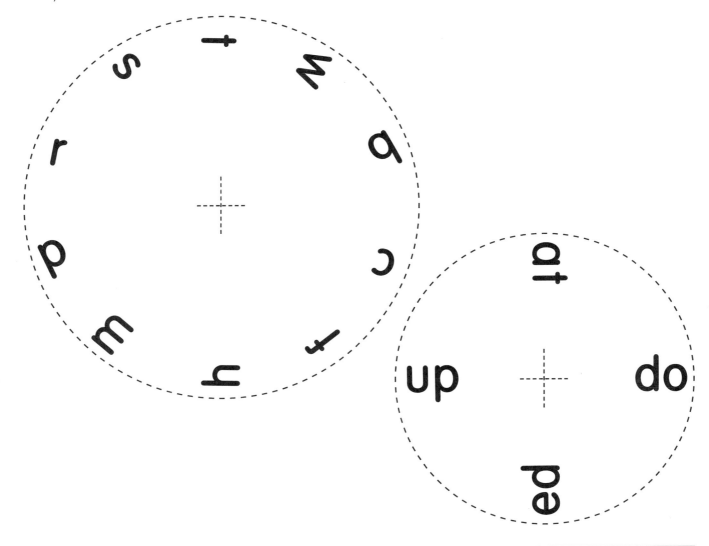

Hand Jive

Directions: Explain to the children that in hand jive you use your hands to make the motions that tell the words of a song or rhyme. Use hand jive to perform the rhyme.

RHYME: Hush-a-bye, Baby

Hush-a-bye, baby, on the treetop,   (Rock an imaginary baby.)
When the wind blows, the cradle will rock;   (Puff out cheeks and blow; rock cradle.)
When the bough bends, the cradle will fall.   (Hold arms overhead, drop arms to side.)
Down will come baby, cradle and all.   (Pretend to catch baby and rock.)

Try some body jive for one of the other "H" rhymes provided below.

RHYME: Hey, Diddle, Diddle
Hey, diddle, diddle,
The cat and the fiddle,
The cow jumped over the moon;
The little dog laughed
To see such sport,
And the dish ran away with the spoon.

RHYME: Humpty Dumpty
Humpty Dumpty sat on a wall.
Humpty Dumpty had a great fall.
All the King's horses and all the King's men
Couldn't put Humpty Dumpty together again.

"H" Is for Half

Directions: Look at the picture halves for the "H" rhymes. Cut out the pictures on pages 48 and 49. To make whole pictures, paste the matching halves onto construction paper. Color each picture. Recite the rhymes on page 47.

48

"H" Is for Half

"I"
Is for Insects

**CHILDREN'S BOOK: Insects Are My Life
Written by Megan McDonald and
illustrated by Paul Brett Johnson**

This story stars a girl who is crazy about insects. "Dozens of bugs. Cousins of bugs. Big bugs. Small bugs. Any bugs. All bugs. Creepy bugs. Crawly bugs. Slimy bugs. Climby bugs. Bugs with wings. Bugs that sing." Amanda Frankenstein loves them all!

After sharing the book *Insects Are My Life*, hold a discussion to find out which children like bugs.

- Do you ever set bugs free?
- Do you ever draw bugs?
- Do you collect dead bugs?
- Do you step around spider webs?
- Do you dream you are an insect?
- Do you like movies about insects?
- Do you pick up live bugs and spiders?

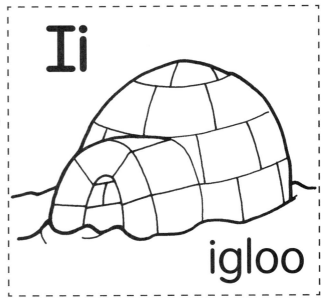

Ii

igloo

SONG: The Insects Go Inching
Sing to the tune of "The Ants Go Marching"

The insects go inching one by one, hurrah, hurrah.
The insects go inching one by one, hurrah, hurrah.
The insects go inching one by one,
The little one stops to suck his thumb.
And they all go inching along the ground.
To get out of the rain, BOOM! BOOM! BOOM!

*Additional verses: Sing lines one through four as stated below.
Repeat lines five and six as shown above.*

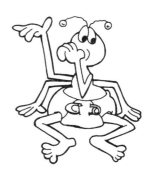

The insects go inching two by two, . . . The little one stops to tie his shoe.
The insects go inching three by three, . . . The little one stops to climb a tree.
The insects go inching four by four, . . . The little one stops to shut the door.
The insects go inching five by five, . . . The little one stops to take a dive.
The insects go inching six by six, . . . The little one stops to pick up sticks.
The insects go inching seven by seven, . . . The little one stops to pray to heaven.
The insects go inching eight by eight, . . . The little one stops to shut the gate.
The insects go inching nine by nine, . . . The little one stops to check the time.
The insects go inching ten by ten, . . . The little one stops to say "THE END."

OUTSIDE ADVENTURE: Insect Search

Have the children take drawing paper and crayons on a hike and look for bugs and other insects. When the children find some insects, they are to draw and color the bugs the appropriate colors. Back in the classroom, invite the children to share their drawings. Try to identify the insects the children drew. Help them write the names of the insects on their pictures.

GAME: Is It Alive?

Name things that begin with the letter I. Have the children move their index fingers along like a worm to indicate "It's a living thing" and hold up their hands like a stop signal to indicate that "It's not living thing." Say the following examples:

- inchworm
- iguana
- igloo
- impala
- insect
- ink
- ibex
- ibis

What are an ibex and an ibis? Write each word on the board. Have the children guess and list the guesses on the board. Look up the animal words in the encyclopedia and show the picture of the ibex (African goat) and the ibis (long-legged wading bird).

LISTENING GAME: The Two Sounds of "I"

Explain that letter I has two sounds—long and short. The long /i/ sound says its name. The short /i/ is the first sound in "ill." List words having the /i/ sound. Have the children indicate the long /i/ by holding hands far apart or the short /i/ by holding thumb and index finger just a small space apart.

Examples:

- ice cream
- inch
- iris
- igloo
- insect
- ibex
- icky
- iguana
- ice
- icicle
- ibis
- ice cube

LEARNING ACTIVITY: Measuring by Inchworm

Reproduce the pattern below onto poster board and cut it out. Each child needs a copy of the inchworm. Pair the children and have them use the inchworms to measure each other's height and the length of their legs, arms, feet, and hands. Direct the children to draw pictures of their partners on paper and list their measurements on the pictures.

Examples:

- My partner is _____ inchworms tall.
- My partner's arm is _____ inchworms long.
- My partner's leg is _____ inchworms long.

Inchworm Pattern

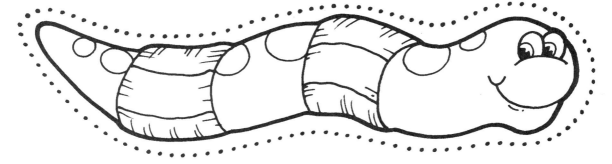

SHADOW BOX BOOK: Ii Page

(See directions on page 7.)

Picture-Word Suggestions—(long vowel sound) ice cube, icicle, ice cream, iris, ivory, iron; (short vowel sound) igloo, iguana, inchworm, insect

It's a Round in Two Parts

RHYME: I Sing, I Sing
I sing, I sing,
From morning till night,
From cares I'm free,
And my heart is light.

Directions: A round is a song sung by groups who begin the song at different times. It is a song that harmonizes with itself. The tricky part is singing words that are different from what you hear others singing. It takes concentration! Singing a round is a lot of fun, but you need to make sure that the children know the words to the song. The singers must focus on what they are singing. If they stumble over the words of the song, they may not be able to keep up with the others. Practice singing the rhyme to the tune of the first four lines of "Twinkle, Twinkle, Little Star." Practice and practice. When everyone knows the words, try singing it as a round. When the first group begins singing the third line of the verse, the second group begins singing the first line. Sing the entire song three times as a round.

Try using the other rhymes below as speaking rounds. When the children know all of the words, have them form two groups. When group one begins the third line, group two begins the first line. Speak in sing-song voices.

RHYME: If All The World
If all the world were water,
And all the water were ink,
What should we do for bread and cheese?
What should we do for drink?

RHYME: Hobby Horse
If I had a hobby horse,
And it was dapple gray,
Its head was made of pea-straw,
And its tail was made of hay.

"I" Collages

Directions: Discuss the idea that a collage is a collection of things that are put together to create a certain impression. Ask the children to think about themselves as a "collage." What are the different things that make them unique? You may want to do a collage of yourself as a sample to show the children. Then give them the pattern for the collage below. Share some of the ideas listed below to get the children started.

1. Write your name and decorate it.
2. Cut and paste pictures of your favorite things.
3. Illustrate things that you like to do.
4. Color or paint the collage with your favorite colors.
5. Ask people to write things about you on it.
6. Attach a photograph of yourself.
7. Attach small items that help describe who you are. For example, a baseball card suggests someone who likes baseball.
8. Draw a picture or attach a photograph of your favorite place.

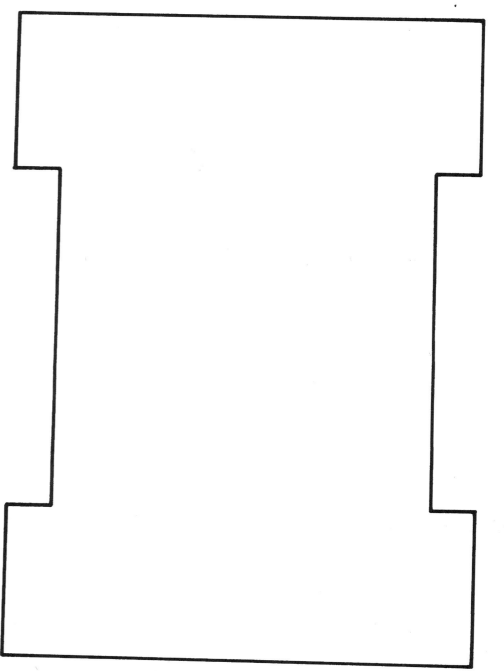

If . . .

Getting Ready: Recite the rhyme with the children. Discuss the meaning of the title.

Directions: Read aloud each rhyme below or make up your own, and let the children use their imaginations to answer the questions. For example:

> **RHYME: If**
> If all the world were water,
> And all the water were ink,
> What should we do for bread and cheese?
> What should we do for drink?

Teacher asks:　　　　If all the world were ice cream,
　　　　　　　　　　　And all the water were root beer,
　　　　　　　　　　　What should we do for dessert?
Children may respond:　We could drink root-beer floats.

If all the rocks were bread,
And all the leaves were slices of cheese,
What should we do for supper?

If all the leaves were dollars,
And all the rocks were quarters,
Where should we keep all our money?

If all the world were artificial grass,
And all the stars were floodlights,
When could we watch a sporting event?

If all the world were feathers,
And all the children could fly,
How could we travel to school?

If all the shoes were skates,
And all the dirt were ice,
What should we do Sunday?

If all the days were Saturday,
And all the seasons were summer,
When could we attend school?

If all the world were laughter,
And all the water were giggles,
What should we do if we sneezed?

If all the world were children,
And no one ever grew old,
What could we do on birthdays?

"J" Is for Jazz and Jelly Beans

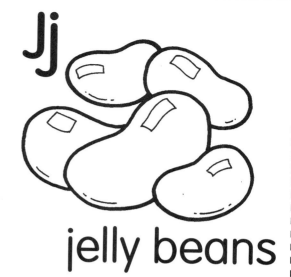

Jj

jelly beans

CHILDREN'S BOOK:
The Jazzy Alphabet
Written by Sherry Shahan and illustrated by Mary Thelen

The Jazzy Alphabet may be the hippest alphabet book ever! It will keep toes tapping from the letter A for alley cat to the letter Z for zoot suit.

CIRCLE TIME: What Letter?

Each page in the book contains a variety of objects that begin with the matching letter of the alphabet. As you read the text and show the pictures, have children point out the appropriate items on each page. Examples: "A"—automobiles, accordion; "B"—bear, bongos

PHONICS: Letter Recognition

As you read the book aloud, stop and have the children identify the main letter for each page. For example: "boogie-woogie, bebop, a boogaloo. Bim-bam blue!" That's the "B" page, that's for sure, but the other letters will not be so easy to identify.

PHONEMIC AWARENESS: Recognizing Letter Sounds

This time when you reread the book, have the children snap fingers, clap hands, or stomp feet each time they hear the sound of the letter for that page. Challenge them to count the number of times a certain letter sound is heard.

MUSIC: Story Rhythm

The rhythm of the story can best be emphasized with music. Provide spoons, coffee cans, pie tins, tissue boxes, cardboard tubes, and clay flowerpots for making musical instruments. (See the directions on page 83.) The children can use the timekeepers, drums, tambourines, strummers, rattles, and clangers to accompany the reading of the story. As you read aloud, use your finger to indicate when the children should play their instruments and how to keep the beat.

Examples:
- A—A-ba-zab-a
- B—Boo-gie-woo-gie be-bop a boog-a-loo. Bim-bam-blue!
- C—Clip-clop clap-pin' hap-pen-in'

LARGE GROUP ACTIVITY: Pairs Performance

Write out the text of the book, with each letter on a different sheet of paper. Divide the pages among pairs of children. Allow time for the children to rehearse their pages. Encourage them to add musical instruments and movements to their performance. Then put it all together by having the children perform their parts in alphabetical order.

CUT AND PASTE: Collages

After looking at the illustrations in the book, the children may be interested in creating their own jazzy alphabet collages. Precut basic shapes (circles, squares, and triangles) and large block letters from construction paper, cellophane, aluminum foil, gold wrapping paper, wallpaper, or newspaper. Encourage the children to choose the shapes and letters they like best, arrange them in a pleasing way, and glue them onto sheets of black construction paper.

BULLETIN BOARD: Decorated Letters

Provide large, precut letters of the alphabet. The children can decorate their selected letters in a way that represents the letter. Example: Polka-dotted "P."

Before starting the project, generate a list of different words that start with certain letters. Provide assistance as needed while the children work. When the letters are decorated, let each child explain his work. Finally, attach the letters to a bulletin board entitled: Jazzy Alphabet! Invite classroom guests to guess the explanation for each letter.

Examples:

A — angled, arched, appetizing
B — blue, black, brown, beaded, bumpy, beautiful
C — checkered, cracked, crunched, crushed
D — dotted, dirty, dim, dazzling, dark, drab, dingy, dark
E — elegant, eel-like, even, edged
F — fancy, fiery, fat, fabric, freckled, fringed, frozen, flat
G — green, gold, gray, gleaming, gingerbread, glossy
H — hairy, huge, hooped, horned
I — ivory, icy, icky
J — jumping, juicy, jagged, jeweled, jumbo, jelly bean
K — kicking, king, knotted
L — long, large, little, ladder, looped
M — mixed-up, music, muddy, mashed, messy
N — nutty, notched, numbered, nest
O — orange, olive, odd, oval, outlined, outer space
P — purple, pink, polka-dotted, plaid, plain, painted, padded, prickly
Q — quirky, quiet, queen, quilted
R — red, roundish, ribbon, ruffled, rough, rusty
S — square, sagging, scary, speckled, smeared, starred, striped, spotted
T — tiny, tough, tan, tangled, triangular, tropical
U — upside down, ugly, unique, unzipped, untidy
V — vine, violet, vivid
W — white, wiggly, wavy, worn, wide
X — eXciting, eXcellent, eXit
Y — yellow, yarn, young, yucky
Z — zany, zippy, zebra-stripped, zigzagged

SHADOW BOX BOOK: Jj Page
(See directions on page 7.)

Picture-Word Suggestions—jaguar, jellybean, jewel, jelly, jar, jellyfish, juice, jacket

---

Jump-Rope Games

Directions: Use the "Jack" rhymes to jump rope. "Jack and Jill" might be the easiest rhyme to use. Have the children jump on every underlined word.

Jack and Jill went up a hill,
To fetch a pail of wa-ter;
Jack fell down and broke his crown,
And Jill came tumbling af-ter.

Variation: Hot pepper rope jumping means to pull the rope under the feet twice on one jump. Recite the rhyme "Jack Be Nimble" and on the word "candlestick," try jumping hot peppers.

Jack be nim-ble; Jack be quick.
Jack jump over the candlestick.

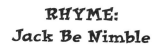

RHYME:
Jack Be Nimble
Jack be nimble; Jack be quick.
Jack jump over the candlestick.

Discussion: Explain syncopation to the children. In syncopation, the offbeats are stressed. When you walk, your feet make a regular beat. When you skip, your feet make a syncopated rhythm. Jumping rope makes regular rhythms, while double Dutch rope jumping is an example of syncopation. For a real challenge, let the children practice syncopation by jumping double Dutch to every word in "Jack Sprat." Two people turn ropes in opposite directions while a third person jumps both ropes. This will take a great deal of practice. Encourage the children who can jump double Dutch to demonstrate syncopated jumping for the other children.

Jack Sprat	could eat	no fat,	
His wife	could eat	no lean,	
And so,	bet-ween	them both,	you see,
They licked	the plat-	ter clean.	

Jazzy Jacks

Directions: Introduce the concept of jazz music to the children. Explain that jazz is a free form, improvised, unique kind of sound. Jazz is a one-of-a-kind musical happening, often invented as the musician performs. Play some jazz music for the children. Then encourage them to practice singing one of the Jack rhymes in a "jazzy" way.

RHYME: **Jack Sprat**
Jack Sprat
Had a cat.
It had but one ear;
It went to buy butter
But butter was dear.

"J" Wall Plaques

Directions: To make a wall plaque to celebrate the letter J, the child can decorate the edges of a paper plate with the letter J. Use paint, washable markers, or crayons to make the letters colorful. Then color and cut out a photocopy of one of the scenes of the Jack rhyme on pages 58–60. Paste the picture in the center of the plate. Put a hole at the top center and add a yarn loop to serve as a hanger.

Jack and Jill went up a hill,
To fetch a pail of water;
Jack fell down and broke his crown,
And Jill came tumbling after.

"J" Wall Plaques

(See directions on page 58.)

**Jack be nimble; Jack be quick.
Jack jump over the candlestick.**

"J" Wall Plaques

(See directions on page 58.)

**Jack Sprat could eat no fat,
His wife could eat no lean,
And so, between them both, you see,
They licked the platter clean.**

"K" Is for Kisses

CHILDREN'S BOOK: Kiss Good Night Written by Amy Hest and illustrated by Anita Jeram

Mrs. Bear is trying to put her son Sam to bed. But no matter what she does, Sam is never quite ready—he's waiting for something. Guess what!

As you read the story, emphasize the hard /k/ sound at the beginning, middle, or end of words. Encourage children to make the hard /k/ sound when they hear it. Examples include the following words: dark, book, blanket, tucking, milk, drank, shook, think, kiss, kissing, and taking.

GAME: The /K/ Sound

The purpose of this game is to identify and reinforce the sound of the letter K by saying certain words. Children will listen and tell if the /k/ sound is at the beginning, middle, or end of the word. Repeat each word several times, emphasizing the /k/ sound. Have the children indicate the location of the sound by touching the top of their heads if the sound is in the beginning of the word, by touching their tummies if the sound is in the middle of the word, or by touching their toes if the sound is at the end of the word. Examples of words are as follows:

- dark
- book
- blanket
- tucking
- milk
- drank
- shook
- think
- kiss
- kite
- ticket
- key

PHONICS: Vowel Recognition

To practice the long and short vowel sounds plus the /k/ sound, rewrite the chant from the story "Jack and the Beanstalk." (fe, fi, fo, fum!)

Chant:

ka (as in cackle), ke (as in kettle), ki (as in kitchen), ko (as in cotton), ku (as in cousin),
I hear the short vowels; do you?
    kA (cake), kE (key), kI (kite), kO (coat), kU (cute),
    I hear the sound of the long vowels, too.

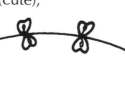

SHADOW BOX BOOK: Kk Page

Picture-Word Suggestions—key, kite, kiss, katydid, ketchup, kettle, keyhole

(See directions on page 7.)

Kaleidoscope of "Ks"

Directions: One way to reinforce the letter K is to make sponge stamp prints in a kaleidoscope of colors. For this project you will need new household sponges, paper, various colors of tempera paint, fine-tip washable markers, scissors, and paper plates.

1. Draw a stencil-shape letter K on a sponge.

2. Cut out the sponge letter.

3. Dampen the sponge stamp with water and squeeze out the excess water so it is pliable.

4. Pour a different color of tempera paint onto each paper plate. Have each child create a kaleidoscope of letter prints by dipping the sponge shape into the paint and stamping the paper in an array of colors.

5. When changing colors of paint, the children should wash out the paint in the sponge shape and squeeze out the excess water.

"K" Was a Kitten

RHYME: K Was a Kitten
K was a kitten
Who jumped at a cork,
And learned to eat mice
Without plate, knife, or fork.

RHYME: Old King Cole
Old King Cole was a merry old soul,
And a merry old soul was he;
And he called for his pipe,
And he called for his bowl,
And he called for his fiddlers three.
And every fiddler, he had a fine fiddle,
And a very fine fiddle had he;
"Tweedle dee, tweedle dee," said the fiddlers:
"Oh, there's none so rare as can compare
With King Cole and his fiddlers three."

ape	newt
bat	ostrich
cow	penguin
dog	quail
elephant	rooster
fox	spider
goat	turkey
hamster	unicorn
inchworm	vulture
jackrabbit	woodpecker
kitten	x-ray fish
lion	yak
mouse	zebra

Directions: Cut apart the alphabet animal cards. Place them in a hat, bowl, or box. The object of this game is for one child to act out one of the animals and for the other children to guess what it is. To play, one child draws a card from the container and hands it to the teacher.

The teacher whispers the name on the card to the child and makes sure the child is familiar with the animal. The child pantomimes or acts out the animal for the other children. (You may want to make this a true charade or allow sound effects.) With very young children it is probably a good idea to review all of the animals before playing the game. Some children might not be familiar with all the animals or their names. If you think that some animals are too obscure for your children, remove those name cards from the game.

For older children who are reading, it may be helpful to write the animal names on the board so that the children can refer to them during the game. Give children 20 to 30 seconds or longer to guess. Determine the length of time that is appropriate for the children.

Name _____

What's That "K" Thing?

Directions: Say the name of each picture. Cut out and glue the correct word in each box below.

koala	kitchen
kangaroo	key

     64   *Learning ABC's Through Literature and Rhymes*

"L"
Is for Ladybugs

Ll

lettuce

CHILDREN'S BOOK:
The Very Lazy Ladybug
Written by Isobel Finn and
illustrated by Jack Tickle

This is a story about a ladybug that is so lazy that she does not learn to fly. Wanting to move about a bit, she hooks rides with animals. She finds no place is quite suitable until finally . . .

As you read the story aloud, encourage the children to determine why the ladybug could not sleep in each place.

Examples:
- kangaroo's pouch—too bumpy
- tiger's back—too noisy
- crocodile's tail—too wet
- monkey's head—made her dizzy
- bear's ear—never sat still
- tortoise's shell—too hot
- elephant's trunk—he sneezed

RECIPE: Peppermint Play Dough

Directions: Mix together $^1/2$ c. (120 mL) cooking oil, 2 c. (470 mL) flour, and 2 c. (470 mL) salt. Stir until smooth. Add a few drops of food coloring and peppermint oil to $^1/2$ c. (120 mL) water and slowly mix it into the other ingredients. The children may be interested in helping you knead the mixture until smooth and pliable.

CRAFT: Peppermint Dough Ladybugs

Use the peppermint dough recipe to make ladybugs. Begin by showing the children how to roll a lump of clay into a smooth ball. Then demonstrate how to press the ball against a firm surface to make a flat bottom on the ladybug shape. Add a tiny ball for the head. Paint the body red with black spots.

CRAFT: Clay Story Animals

Invite the children to create the other animals out of clay or play dough for the literacy corner. When the clay forms are dry, encourage the children to use the animals when retelling the story.

SHADOW BOX BOOK: Ll Page   (See directions on page 7.)
Picture-Word Suggestions—ladybug, leg, ladder, leopard, lightning, lamb, lamp, lock

"L" Rhymes

RHYME: Little Bo Peep
Little Bo Peep has lost her sheep,
And can't tell where to find them;
Let them alone, and they'll come home,
And bring their tails behind them.

RHYME: Ladybug, Ladybug
Ladybug, ladybug, fly away home.
Your house is on fire, your children all gone,
All but one, and her name is Ann,
And she crept out under the pudding pan.

RHYME: Little Jack Horner
Little Jack Horner
Sat in a corner,
Eating a Christmas pie;
He put in his thumb,
And pulled out a plum,
And said, "What a good boy am I!"

RHYME: Little Boy Blue
Little boy blue, come blow your horn;
The sheep's in the meadow; the cow's in the corn.
Where's the little boy that looks after the sheep?
He's under the haystack, fast asleep.

Let's Create New Lyrics

Directions: Explain to the children that lyrics are words set to music. Matching the number of notes to the number of syllables is the important thing to remember when writing lyrics. Sometimes lyrics rhyme, but they do not have to. One easy way to have children create lyrics is to change words in a familiar poem or song.

In small groups, have children make up new lyrics for an "L" rhyme. For example:

Little Lynn Willow
Sat on a pillow,
Eating a lemon cake.
She put in her thumb,
And pulled out some gum,
And said, "What a great mistake!"

Name _____

Lovely Literature

Directions: Use stamps of "L" words on this page to complete the rebus story on pages 68 and 69. Cut out and glue the stamps in the story. The pictures you choose to use will make your story different from everyone else's story. Not every stamp is needed. Just use the ones you like the best.

Name _____

Lovely Literature

Once upon a time, two friends,

a [____] and a [____], went for

a walk. They found a [____] to

eat. They also found a [____] to

eat. They laughed as they lunched

while sitting on a [____].

Name _____

Later, a ⬚ saw the two

friends eating. "How can you eat

those things?" it asked.

"I like ⬚ ."

The two friends shook their heads

and smiled, "We like this lunch."

"M" Is for Madeline and Market Street

CHILDREN'S BOOK: Madeline
Written and illustrated
by Ludwig Bemelmans

This storybook offers children a chance to see famous European spots. Madeline includes illustrations of the Eiffel Tower, the Paris Opera, the Place Vendôme, Notre Dame de Paris, plus more. Other Madeline books in the series:

- *Madeline and the Bad Hat*
- *Madeline's Rescue*
- *Madeline and the Gypsies*
- *Madeline in London*

After reading each page aloud, have the children find Madeline and her whereabouts.

CHILDREN'S BOOK: On Market Street
Written by Arnold Lobel and illustrated by Anita Lobel

On Market Street is described on the flap as a world of wonders from "A" to "Z." When the Market Street merchants open their doors, there is plenty to see. Inspired by seventeenth-century French trade engravings, the vibrant paintings will provide hours of fun as readers go on a memorable "shopping spree."

CIRCLE TIME: Market Street Shopping

Getting Ready: Prepare for this activity by collecting the 26 objects that were bought on Market Street: apple, book, clock, doughnut, egg, flower, glove, hat, ice cream, jewel, kite, lollipop, musical instrument, noodle, orange, playing card, quilt, ribbon, shoe, toy, umbrella, vegetable, wig, X-mas tree, yarn, and zipper.

Directions: Pass the objects out among the children—some may have several, depending upon the class size. As you read the book aloud, the child with the appropriate object stands, holds it up, and then quietly sits. After reading the book, review the sounds of letters A–M. Example: Name the Market Street object that begins with the letter M.

Game: Divide the class into three groups. Randomly place the 26 objects on a table. One at a time, using the book as a reference, have each group arrange the objects in alphabetical order. Afterward, place the book and objects in the learning center so children can practice putting them in alphabetical order.

(Patterns for the Market Street items are on page 71.)

Phonemic Awareness: Letter-Sound Recognition

Reproduce the Market Street cards (below) onto card stock for each child. You may wish to enlarge the pictures before making the photocopies. Cut apart the cards. Children can color the pictures and write the appropriate uppercase and lowercase letter on the back of each card. Use the picture cards to review the sounds of letters and ABC order.

SHADOW BOX BOOK: Mm Page (See directions on page 7.)

Picture-Word Suggestions—man, mat, me, mother, money, monkey, moose, mouse, moon, mushroom, muffin, mask, mug, mountain

---

Market Street Card Patterns

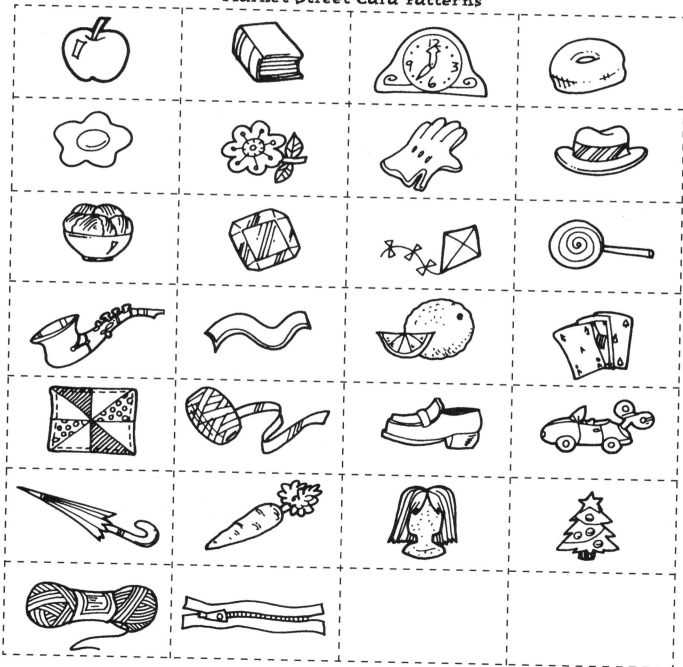

Mary Had a Little Monkey

RHYME: Mary Had a Little Lamb

Mary had a little lamb
With fleece as white as snow,
And everywhere that Mary went
The lamb was sure to go.

It followed her to school one day,
That was against the rule;
It made the children laugh and play,
To see the lamb at school.

Directions: Practice singing the first two original verses. Then sing and substitute "M" animals for the word lamb. When singing these new verses, you may be interested in having the children use the puppet patterns on page 73.

Mary had a little monkey
With fur as white as snow,
And everywhere that Mary went
The monkey was sure to go.

It followed her to school one day,
That was against the rule;
It made the children laugh and play,
To see a monkey at school.

Mary had a musical moose;
It could sing and dance, you know,
And everywhere that Mary went
The moose was sure to go.

It followed her to school one day,
That was against the rule;
It made the children laugh and play,
To see a moose at school.

Mary had a giant mule,
It wore a big blue bow,
And everywhere that Mary went
The mule was sure to go.

It followed her to school one day,
That was against the rule;
It made the children laugh and play,
To see a mule at school.

Mary's Puppet Patterns

Directions: Copy, color, and cut out the animal faces. Attach each one to a craft stick with tape. The children can use the puppets while singing the new verses found on page 72.

Name _____

Directions: Look at each animal. Can you see what body part is missing? Draw on the missing body parts and color the animals.

What's Missing?

Missing: the monkey's mouth, the alligator's arm, the cat's tail, and the elephant's eyes

KE-804020 © Key Education   74   *Learning ABC's Through Literature and Rhymes*

"N" Is for Nose and Nonsense

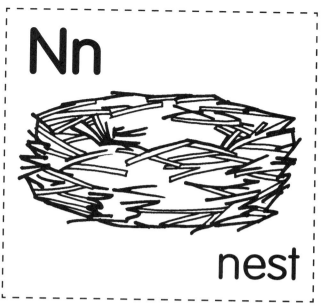

CHILDREN'S BOOK: Arthur's Nose
Written and illustrated by Marc Brown

Arthur is unhappy with his nose, so what is he going to do about it? After trying on all kinds of noses, Arthur decides that his nose fits the best.

Read *Arthur's Nose* aloud. After sharing the book, look at each picture and find things that begin with the letter N.

PHONEMIC AWARENESS: Nose Hum

Demonstrate the /n/ sound. Just for fun, ask the children to pinch their nostrils and make the sound for the letter N. Show the alphabet card above while making this sound. Follow up the activity by naming parts of the body and having the children make the "nose hum" signal when they hear an N word.

Examples:

- nose
- nails
- eyes
- neck
- foot
- toes
- elbow
- arm
- nostrils

CHILDREN'S BOOK: Chicka, Chicka, Boom, Boom
Written by Bill Martin Jr. and John Archambault and illustrated by Lois Ehlert

After reading the book through once, give each child an index card with a letter of the alphabet printed on it. If you have made a set of alphabet picture cards (one card shown above) using the patterns provided in this book, then distribute those cards to the children. Have the children hold their cards facing you. As you reread the book, instead of saying each letter, point to the person holding that specific letter. He is to say his letter in a creative way. Give children time to make up unique ways of saying their letters. Then with group participation, present the story.

Examples:

A—in very deep voice
B—stretch the sound for a long time, Beeeeeeeeee.
C—in a very high pitch like an opera singer
D—dadadada De
E—Eeeeeeeeeeeeeeeee

SHADOW BOX BOOK: Nn Page
(See directions on page 7.)

Picture-Word Suggestions—nails, nuts, needle, nose, nest, net, nine, notebook, newspaper, nostrils, nickel, number, necktie

---

Ends with "N"?

Name _____

Directions: Say the name of each animal. Can you hear the N sound at the end of the word? Circle yes or no.

yes no	yes no	yes no
yes no	yes no	yes no
yes no	yes no	yes no

Sing a Nightingale's Song

> **RHYME: The Nightingale Sings**
> The nightingale sings when we're at rest;
> The nightingale sings when we're at rest;
> The little bird climbs the tree for its nest,
> With a hop, step, and a jump.

Directions: Turn the rhyme into a group participation song with the sounds and actions below. Assign speaking parts to individuals or small groups. Every time a certain word is spoken, the individual or group makes the appropriate sound. Then have the children recite the rhyme while participating with sound effects and actions.

nightingale   (*tweedy dee, tweedy dee*)
sings   (*tweet, tweet*)
rest   (*snoring sounds*)
bird   (*chirp, chirp*)
tree   (*swish, swish*)
Everyone does the hop, step, and jump.

Alternative: Use actions to learn the following rhyme.

The North Wind doth blow,   (*Wrap arms around body.*)
We soon shall have snow,   (*Wiggle fingers overhead like snow.*)
And what will the robin do then,   (*Shrug shoulders, shake head slowly.*)
     Poor thing.   (*Sigh!*)

He'll sit in a barn,   (*Form barn roof with hands overhead.*)
And keep himself warm,   (*Wrap arms around body.*)
And hide his head under his wing,   (*Put head under one arm.*)
     Poor thing.   (*Sigh!*)

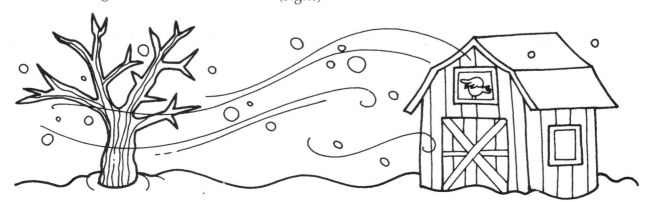

Papier-Mâché "N"

RHYME: "N" Was a Nosegay

"N" was a nosegay,
Sprinkled with dew,
Pulled in the morning
And presented to you.

It is easy for children to make papier-mâché letters. Be sure to have all the supplies available. You may want to complete steps 1–4 for each child.

1. Roll an 8.5 in. x 11 in. (22 cm x 28 cm) piece of paper.

2. Divide the paper roll into three equal parts and bend it to make the letter N. This is the base. Place it on several layers of newspaper.

3. Rip newspaper into strips about 1 in. (25 mm) wide.

4. Mix $1/2$ c. (120 mL) flour with 1 tbsp. (15 mL) salt and 1 c. (240 mL) warm water to make a thin paste.

5. Have the children dip the newspaper strips into the paste and layer them over the N shape. Wrap them around all of the edges. Make sure the letter can stand independently.

6. When the papier-mâché is dry and ready to be painted, it will feel hard to the touch. A day is usually long enough to dry small papier-mâché objects.

7. When completely dry, paint and decorate the letter with markers, glitter, and stickers.

North Wind Doth Blow

Name _____

Directions: Poor Robin keeps warm by hopping into the barn. Where do the other animals keep warm in the winter? Draw a line to match each animal with its home. Color the animals and their homes.

RHYME: The North Wind
The North Wind doth blow.
We soon shall have snow,
And what will the robin do then?

A New Nose

Directions: To celebrate the /n/ sound as in "nose" and the sense of smell, conduct a discussion about noses and create a small classroom bulletin board. Begin by covering the bulletin board with white paper. With a washable, black marker, write a title and the nose rhyme on the board. To complete the display, have the children cut out large faces and noses from old magazines.

> **RHYME: Nose, Nose**
> Nose, nose, jolly red nose;
> And what gave you that jolly red nose?
> Nutmeg and cinnamon, spices and cloves,
> And they gave me this jolly red nose.

Paste a new nose on each face and attach it to the board. Try to cover the board with a collage of faces. Discuss how different people look with new noses. Examine all of the noses on the bulletin board and let the class choose the funniest nose, most interesting nose, most beautiful nose, largest nose, tiniest nose, and so on. Discuss the sense of smell. Find out what aroma children enjoy smelling the most. Create a class list of favorite smells. Who likes the smell of cookies baking? Hard-boiled eggs? Lemons? Burning rubber? Skunks? Wet dogs? Roses?

Nose, nose, jolly red nose;
And what gave you that jolly red nose?
Nutmeg and cinnamon, spices and cloves.
And they gave me this jolly red nose.

"O" Is for Opposites and Olivia

Oo

ostrich

CHILDREN'S BOOK: The Foot Book:
Dr. Seuss's Wacky Book of Opposites
Written and illustrated by Dr. Seuss

This storybook is a delightful way to introduce and reinforce opposites, such as left and right, high and low, front and back, and small and big.

CIRCLE TIME: Sorting

To introduce the concepts of small and large, bring in a variety of shoes, including baby shoes. Have the children sort the shoes into two piles and also line them up according to size.

GAME: Visual Memory

Reinforce visual memory with this game. Name two animals. The children tell which one is small and which one is large.

- bug—elephant
- bat—whale
- horse—mouse
- cat—tiger
- turtle—lion
- spider—giraffe

RECIPE: Sweet and Sour

Make a sweet and sour snack by dipping banana rings into orange gelatin. For this activity provide plastic serrated knives, bananas, orange gelatin, waxed paper, and paper cups. Have each child peel a banana, place it on waxed paper, and slice it into rings. Pour a small spoonful of gelatin in each paper cup for the children. Direct the child to dip an edge of a sweet banana slice into the sour orange gelatin. Discuss how sweet and sour (tart) are opposites.

LARGE GROUP ACTIVITY: Opposites

Name one of the words for a pair of opposites. Ask the children to think of the other word.

- yes—no
- day—night
- thick—thin
- loud—quiet
- hot—cold
- sweet—sour
- girl—boy
- light—heavy
- up—down
- smooth—rough
- work—play
- small—large
- in—out
- happy—sad
- some—none
- wet—dry
- black—white
- tall—short
- few—lots

PHONICS: Letter Recognition

The letter O is round. What else is round? As you name things, each child may identify those things that are round by saying "Ohhhhhhh" and making a circle with a thumb and index finger.
Examples:

- box
- nickel
- basketball
- doughnut
- heart
- envelope
- crayon
- zero
- wheel
- orange
- snowball
- stamp
- shoe
- baseball bat
- olive
- ring
- sock
- pickle

 Learning ABC's Through Literature and Rhymes

CHILDREN'S BOOK: Olivia
Written and illustrated by Ian Falconer

Olivia is a pig with high energy and strong self-esteem. "This is Olivia. She is good at lots of things." Olivia may be a pig, but that does not stop her from dreaming of becoming a ballerina. One or two lines of text per page make this a book some children will want to learn to read all by themselves. Other Olivia books to share with your class include:

- *Olivia and the Missing Toy*
- *Teatro Olivia*
- *Olivia on the Go*
- *Olivia's Opposites*
- *Olivia Saves the Circus*
- *Dream Big (with attitude)*

Read the story aloud without pausing for comments. Then find out what your children have in common with Olivia. Pause to ask questions, such as the following:
- Olivia is good at lots of things. What can you do well?
- Olivia wears people out. Do you?
- Is there someone who tells you that you wear them out? Who?
- Olivia has a little brother? Do you have a little brother or sister? Does he/she copy you?
- Olivia has a dog and cat? Do you have a pet? Tell us about your pet.
- When Olivia gets dressed, she likes to try on everything. Do you ever do that?
- Olivia likes the beach. Do you?
- Olivia likes to build sand castles. Do you?
- Olivia does not like taking a nap. Do you like napping?
- Olivia likes the museum. Which museum do you like the best?
- Olivia likes to hear bedtime stories. Does someone read bedtime stories to you?
- What is your favorite bedtime story?

LEARNING CENTER: Sand Castles

Set up a sand-castle center in your classroom. Place a small plastic wading pool on a table. Fill it with four to six bags of sand. Provide plastic cups, bowls, and spoons for molding wet sand. Place a pail of water next to the sand-castle center. Watch imaginations soar as the children sculpt objects in the sand.

LEARNING CENTER: Red Dress-Up Corner

Olivia's favorite color is red. Set up an Olivia dress-up center with a full-length mirror and oodles and oodles of red clothes. Ask the children to bring in red articles of clothing: hats, scarves, boots, cloaks, vests, sunglasses, purses, and raincoats. Place them in a large box near the full-length mirror. Alternatively, collect blue or yellow clothes for the dress-up center.

SHADOW BOX BOOK: Oo Page   (See directions on page 7.)

Picture-Word Suggestions—(long vowel sound) oats, oval, opal, ocean, opossum, oatmeal; (short vowel sound) octopus, ostrich, olives, ox, ocelot, otter

---

Old Mother Hubbard's Cupboard Band

Directions: Use things found in the kitchen cupboard to make musical instruments. After children create the instruments, have them use their new music makers to accompany the rhyme.

Spoon Timekeepers

Tap the rounded part of two metal spoons together in time to music. Try tapping the handles together for a different sound. Tie two spoons together with a bit of yarn at the base of the rounded part of the spoon to make a castanet.

Coffee-Can Drum

Try beating the bottom of a coffee can with a spoon. Try drumming it with your fingers. Which sound do you like best? Glue construction paper to the side of the can to decorate the drum. Decorate the paper with washable markers, rickrack, and stickers.

Pie-Tin Tambourine

To make a tambourine, you need a thin foil pie tin. Use a pencil to punch holes around the edges of the pan. Attach a jingle bell, paper clip, or any other small metal object to each hole with yarn.

Tissue-Box Strummer

Use different sized rubber bands stretched around an empty tissue box to make a great sound. Be sure to space the rubber bands evenly over the hole in the top of the tissue box.

Tissue-Roll Rattle

Place aluminum foil on one end of a bathroom tissue cardboard tube and secure it with tape or a rubber band. Pour rice, beans, or macaroni into the tube. Cover the other end with aluminum foil and secure it. Decorate the shaker with washable markers and stickers.

Clay-Pot Clanger

Tie a nut or bolt to a piece of yarn. String the yarn through the hole in the bottom of a clay flowerpot. Then inside the pot, tape the yarn to the top of the pot to secure the bolt clapper. Decorate with washable watercolor markers.

Old MacDonald's Old Timer's Band

RHYME: Old MacDonald Had a Farm
Old MacDonald had a farm—E-I-E-I-O.
And on that farm he had a pig—E-I-E-I-O.
With an oink, oink, here and an oink, oink, there.
Here an oink. There an oink.
Everywhere an oink, oink.
Old MacDonald had a farm—E-I-E-I-O.

Getting Ready: Practice the familiar song "Old MacDonald Had a Farm" as a group. When everyone knows the words, introduce the animal cards on pages 85 and 86. Color, cut out, and laminate the cards. Hold up each card and have the children practice making each animal sound and singing each new verse.

Directions: Display the animal cards in the order you want the children to sing the verses. For example, if the picture of a dog is shown, replace the word "pig" with "dog" and the word "oink" with "bowwow" to create a new verse. Practice singing the verses. The picture cards will help the children remember the order of animal sounds as they repeat each of the previously named animals at the end of every verse.

Variation: Use Old Mother Hubbard's Cupboard Band instruments (see page 83) or classroom instruments to add interesting rhythmic patterns or sound effects. When the class knows the song, and can accompany it with instruments, find an audience and perform!

bowwow

squeak

baa

bow-wow

moo

baa

hissssssss

squeak

ri-bit

cluck

hee-haw

honk

meow

oink

neigh

"P"
Is for Pizza and Pigs

CHILDREN'S BOOK:
The Princess and the Pizza
Written by Mary Jane and
illustrated by Herm Auch

Paulina, a true princess, and eleven others vie for the hand of Prince Drupert. As the contest heats up, the competition narrows. *The Princess and the Pizza* takes a lighthearted look at career choices for princesses.

Read the story aloud without pausing for discussion. Then reread it aloud again. This time when children hear a word that begins with the letter P, they are to make that explosive /p/ sound.

CUT AND PASTE: Paper Pizzas

Getting Ready: Cut out a large brown circle from construction paper to represent the pizza crust and a red sauce shape for each child.

Directions: The children are to glue the paper sauce shape on the brown paper crusts. Then have them cut out magazine pictures of P objects and paste them onto their pizzas. When the pizzas are completed, the children can take turns telling the names of their pizzas by including all of the featured objects, such as penguin-partridge-pig-pineapple-pepper pizza. Write the name of each pizza on the board and save the list for the next activity.

LARGE GROUP ACTIVITY:
Tongue-Twister Pizzas

Read the names of the pizzas and use them as tongue twisters. Who can quickly say, "penguin-partridge-pig-pineapple-pepper pizza" three times?

RECIPE: English Muffin Pizzas

Make individual pizzas with English muffins. (Check for food allergies before making the snack for the children.) Provide pizza sauce, bowls of different kinds of grated cheeses, pepperoni and salami slices, pineapple chunks, and olives. Let the children spread the sauce on their own muffins and layer them with their favorite toppings. Warm the individual pizzas in a microwave until the cheese melts.

CHILDREN'S BOOK: A Pig Named Perrier
Written by Elizabeth Spurr and illustrated by Martin Matje

This story is a perfect way to teach and reinforce the letter P. "Perrier is no ordinary pig. He is a purebred potbellied pig." However, Perrier, who is treated like a prince, just is not happy. What will make Perrier happy?

As you read the story, hold up each page and challenge the children to identify P objects. Help them find the following illustrations: pythons, parrot cage, Petunia's Pet Shop, potbellied pig, pineapple, "Little Pigs" book, pink umbrella, piglets, puddle, parlor, Paris, and the Parisian film director.

LARGE GROUP ACTIVITY: Guessing Game

To reinforce the initial consonant sound of P, play a guessing game. Give clues as children guess the words.

- A huge snake (python)
- A talking bird (parrot)
- A place that sells animals (pet store)
- A certain kind of pig (potbellied)
- A tropical fruit (pineapple)
- A very light red color (pink)
- A color made by mixing blue and red (purple)
- Another name for baby pigs (piglets)
- A collection of water on the ground (puddle)
- A place in France (Paris)

PHONICS: Letter Recognition

After introducing the guessing game, have the children give clues for "P" words while the rest of the class tries to guess the words.

SHADOW BOX BOOK: Pp Page   (See directions on page 7.)
Picture-Word Suggestions—panda, pig, pizza, pansies, pear, peach, pie, pin, pen, pony, pot, pop, pumpkin, puppy, peacock, peanut, penny

---

Pink Pudding Painting

RHYME: Pat-a-Cake, Pat-a-Cake
Pat-a-cake, pat-a-cake, baker's man!
Make me a cake as fast as you can:
Pat it, and prick it, and mark it with a "B,"
And there will be enough for Baby and me.

Directions: Writing will be fun when children use pink pudding paint. To make this edible paint, provide strawberry instant pudding (or vanilla pudding with red food coloring), milk, mixing bowl, and spoon. Mix the instant pudding as directed on the back of the package. Chill it until set. Use the pudding paint the way you would use any other finger paint. It is recommended that you have children cover their work area with newspapers before they begin painting. Give each child a large sheet of finger-painting paper and a small paper cup of pudding. Encourage the children to use the pudding to print some words that begin with the letter P. Display a list of words where children can see them as they are writing. Examples of words include pancake, pie, peanut, pecan, peppermint, pepper, pickle, popcorn, pudding, peanut butter, pear, peach, pastry, and pasta.

RHYME: Pease Porridge Hot
Pease porridge hot,
Pease porridge cold,
Pease porridge in the pot nine days old.
Some like it hot,
Some like it cold,
Some like it in the pot nine days old.

Pease Porridge Clapping Game

Directions: Present the rhyme by reading it once to the class. Ask if anyone knows what pease porridge is. Explain that pease is an old-fashioned way of spelling peas. Porridge is very thick soup. Thus, pease porridge is pea soup. Let the children recite the rhyme with you. Repeat as a choral reading. One group says the first and fourth lines. Another group says the second and fifth lines. Everyone says the third and sixth lines of the rhyme. Alternatively, the children can play a clapping game. To play, each child will need to sit facing a partner and perform the following actions:

Pease porridge hot,	(*Slap knees, clap, clap partner's hands.*)
Pease porridge cold,	(*Slap knees, clap, clap partner's hands.*)
Pease porridge in the pot	(*Slap knees, clap, clap partner's right hand, clap.*)
nine days old.	(*Clap partner's left hand, clap, clap partner's hands.*)
Some like it hot,	(*Slap knees, clap, clap partner's hands.*)
Some like it cold,	(*Slap knees, clap, clap partner's hands.*)
Some like it in the pot	(*Slap knees, clap, clap partner's right hand, clap.*)
nine days old.	(*Clap partner's left hand, clap, clap partner's hands.*)

Peter Piper Puppets

RHYME: Peter Piper

Peter Piper picked a peck
Of pickled peppers;
A peck of pickled peppers
Peter Piper picked;

If Peter Piper picked a peck
Of pickled peppers,
Where's the peck of pickled peppers
Peter Piper picked?

Directions: Practice saying the tongue twister *Peter Piper.* Talk about the /p/ sound as in "Peter" and other words that begin with that sound. Then create and use puppets to say tongue twisters. Directions for making a variety of puppets follow. If appropriate, set up a learning table with a sample of each kind of puppet and the necessary supplies and let the children choose which kind of puppet they want to make. Supplies for making puppets include butcher paper, washable markers, old socks, craft glue, beads, bits of felt, feathers, precut red and pink felt tongues, peanuts in shells, yarn, lunch sacks, craft sticks, newspapers, tape, string, cotton, straws, toothpicks, plastic spoons, chenille stems, cloth, vegetables, fruits, raisins, paper plates, and scissors.

Hand Puppets

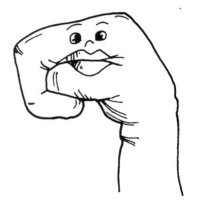

1. Make a fist. Be sure that the thumb is tucked under the fingers as shown.
2. Draw two eyes and a nose on the base of the forefinger with a black washable marker. Use a red washable marker to draw lips around the gap between the fingers and thumb.
3. Repeat on the other hand. Let your hands have a conversation with each other.

Sock Puppets

1. If you are right-handed, put the sock on your left hand. If you are left-handed, put the sock on your right hand.
2. Push the sock in between your thumb and the rest of your hand to make a mouth.
3. Use craft glue to attach beads, felt cutouts, and feathers to complete the puppet's face.
4. Attach a felt tongue. Put glue on the base of the tongue and place it deep inside the puppet's mouth. Let it dry.

Paper Bag Puppets

1. Fill the bag with wadded-up newspapers and tie it with a string.
2. Copy, cut out, and paste some of the facial features on page 92 onto the bag.
3. Decorate the puppet with felt cutouts, paper cutouts, yarn for hair, feathers, and markers.
4. Place your hand inside the bag.

Peter Piper Puppets

Paper Plate Puppets

1. Tape a craft stick to the back of a paper plate.
2. Decorate the front of the plate with paper cutouts, markers, crayons, paints, and felt scraps.
3. Glue on hats, ears, whiskers, and hair.
   These puppets can be held in front of the face and used as masks, too.

Fruit and Vegetable Puppets

(This activity is not recommended for very young children.)

1. Use toothpicks to stick raisins, bits of other vegetables, or felt cutouts to vegetables or fruits.
2. You can draw on some foods with water-based markers.
3. Cut a slit in the bottom of the fruit or vegetable and insert a craft stick handle.
4. Glue little strips of cloth around the bottom of the fruit to hide your hand and handle. Vegetables and fruits make really funny-shaped heads!

Lunch-Bag Puppets

1. Use lunch sacks to make puppets. Draw the mouth where the bottom of the sack meets the side of the sack as illustrated.
2. Decorate the puppet with paper cutouts, fabric scraps, cotton, buttons, ribbons, yarn and string, seeds or noodles, chenille stems, feathers, straws or toothpicks, and wire.

Spoon Puppets

1. Draw a face on a plastic spoon. Glue on yarn hair, whiskers, beard, or mustache.
2. Use chenille stems for arms.
3. Tie a bow around the base of a spoon for a bow tie.
4. Decorate the puppet with paper hats or ears.

Peanut Shell Puppets

(Note: This activity is not recommended for very young children. Be sure the children are not allergic to peanuts.)

1. Carefully crack open some peanuts. (You may eat the peanuts as you crack the shells.) Use the largest half of the shells for your puppets.
2. Draw a face on each shell. Add bits of yarn for hair, beard, and a mustache.
3. Decorate the peanut shell puppets any way you wish, such as with paper hats. Make each puppet different.

Peter Piper Puppet Patterns

"Q" Is for Quack and Quilt

CHILDREN'S BOOK:
Giggle, Giggle, Quack
Written by Doreen Cronin and illustrations by Betsy Lewin

This book is guaranteed to make your children smile. When Farmer Brown goes on vacation, he leaves his brother Bob in charge. Farmer's notes of instruction sometimes seem unlikely, but Bob follows them to the letter. If the children enjoy this book, also share *Click, Clack, Moo: Cows That Type* by the same author.

After sharing the hilarious story, encourage the children to share personal experiences when they were left with a baby-sitter or grandparent and got to do fun things.

LARGE GROUP ACTIVITY: Ducks Quack

Animals make all kinds of sounds. Give animal sounds and have children name the animals.

- howl (wolf)
- bleats (lamb, calf)
- buzz (fly, bee)
- neigh (horse)
- crow (rooster)
- honk (goose)
- growl (dog, bear)
- sing (bird)
- meow (cat)
- roar (lion)
- bray (donkey, hippo)
- squeak (mouse)
- squawk (parrot, gull)
- peep (chicken)
- moo (cow)
- bark (dog)
- gobble (turkey)
- croak (frog)
- hiss (snake)
- grunt (pig)

CHILDREN'S BOOK: Quilt Alphabet
Written by Lesa Cline-Ransome and illustrated by James E. Ransome

Publishers Weekly calls it, "A blue-ribbon ABC book that combines bright, folksy oil paintings and lilting riddle-poems." Before reading each page, say the letter. Show the picture and ask a child to name the object of each page. For example: Ask, "what color is the letter "A"?

BULLETIN BOARD: Quilt

Getting Ready: Cover a 6 ft. (1.8 m) square bulletin board or wall space with black paper. Reproduce the quilt block pattern (page 94) 27 times. Using the book as an example, draw each letter in the center of one of the sheets. Complete the 27th block with a title such as: Our Class' Alphabet Quilt—the first block for the quilt.

Directions: Explain that quilts have patterns of colors and show examples. The children then color the individual blocks like quilt pieces. Prepare 27 solid-color squares, too. Alternating blocks with solid colored squares, just like a quilt, attach them to the bulletin board in six rows of nine blocks. The paper quilt will end up being 66 in. x 67.5 in. (1.65 m x 1.68 m) so center it on your 72 in. (1.80 m) board.

SHADOW BOX BOOK: Qq Page
Picture-Word Suggestions—quilt, quarter, queen, quail
See directions on page 7.)

94

"Q" Is the Queen

RHYME: The Queen of Hearts

The Queen of Hearts,
She made some tarts,
All on a summer's day.
The Knave of Hearts,
He stole the tarts
And took them clean away.

The King of Hearts
Called for the tarts,
And beat the Knave full sore.
The Knave of Hearts
Brought back the tarts,
And vowed he'd steal no more.

Queen of Q Kingdom

RHYME: "Q" Is the Queen

"Q" is the Queen
Who governs the land,

And sits on a throne
Very lofty and grand.

Directions: Increase communication skills with this circle-time game. Choose someone to be the "Queen" (or "King"). That person sits in a chair at the head of the class. Everyone says the rhyme. The Queen (or King) then asks a question of one child. Example: Can you wiggle your ears? The person answers truthfully. Then the Queen asks, "Will you show us?" or "Will you try?" If the person says, "Yes," and demonstrates, she becomes the new queen. If the person says, "No," the Queen turns to another child and asks a new question. If the Queen/King has trouble thinking of questions to ask, give them one of the following:

- Can you whistle?
- Can you crow like a rooster?
- Can you skip?
- Can you hop on one leg?
- Can you walk backwards?
- Can you sing like an opera star?
- Can you count to 10?
- Can you name a word that begins with the letter Q?
- Can you clap five times fast?
- Can you turn a somersault?
- Can you stand on your head?
- Can you run in circles?
- Can you touch your toes?
- Can you spell your name?
- Can you point to something red?
- Can you name three people in the room?
- Can you write an uppercase Q on the chalkboard?

"Q" Is for Quiet Times

Getting Ready: Talk about what each child likes to do during quiet moments. Discuss how wonderful it is to be calm, quiet, and relaxed.

Directions: Do some quiet exercises with the children. Examples: I am as quiet as a caterpillar. (Everyone wiggles quietly on the floor like a caterpillar.) I am as gentle as a baby kitten. (Everyone purrs softly.) I am as tender as a teddy bear. (Everyone rocks softly back and forth and hugs himself.) I am as soft as a baby lamb. (The children feel how soft their hair is.) I am as smooth as a newborn seal. (The children feel their own skin and discover how soft and pliable it is.) Finally, invite the children to work in pairs and help each other relax. Encourage deep and slow breathing. Turn off the lights and play soft, quiet music. Emphasize that this is a quiet time for relaxing.

Variation: Have each child stretch out on his back so that his body is not touching anyone else's. While the lights are off and music is playing softly in the background, offer quiet suggestions that help children relax from the tips of their toes to the tops of their heads. Example: Wiggle just your toes. Now make them be relaxed. They are completely without stress. Your feet are quiet. They feel heavy as if they are made of lead. Your ankles are relaxed.

Move up the body mentioning each body part and help the children become totally relaxed. After you have quieted their entire bodies, invite them for a "ride" on an imaginary elevator going up, up, up into the clouds where they can float freely for a few minutes. When the youngsters are feeling completely relaxed, suggest that they can relax themselves in the same way by beginning with their toes and calming each body part. Help them come out of this totally relaxed state slowly and in stages. Turn off the music. Turn on the lights. Allow the children to remain quiet as long as they choose. Others can be dismissed to go outside or to another part of the room so that they do not disturb those who choose to remain quiet a bit longer.

"R"
Is for Rainbows

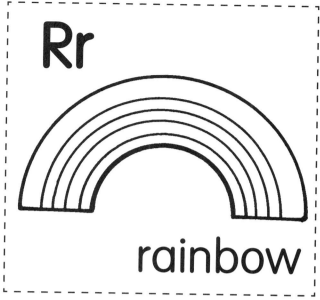

CHILDREN'S BOOK:
Planting a Rainbow
Written and illustrated by Lois Ehlert

This book is about planting a flower garden. In the autumn, bulbs are planted. Winter is a time for ordering from seed catalogs. In the spring, seeds are planted and the bulbs sprout. Summertime is the best of all seasons—a time for watching one's garden turn into a rainbow. Bring a fresh, mixed bouquet to class. Read *Planting a Rainbow* aloud.

What children have flowers that bloom in their yards? Let the children describe the flowers—colors, sizes, shapes. Give each child a flower from the fresh bouquet. Using the pictures of flowers in *Planting a Rainbow*, try to name some of the real flowers. Follow up with the coloring sheet on page 98.

CRAFT: Flowerpot

Getting Ready: Make flowerpots from large foam cups. Use pinking sheers to cut colorful scraps of fabric into 2 in. (5 cm) squares. Prepare a glue mixture of 50% water and 50% craft glue.

Directions:
1. Poke a drain hole in the bottom of each cup with a pencil.
2. Using a paintbrush, apply the glue mixture onto the outside of the cup and press on fabric squares.
3. Repeat, overlapping the squares a bit, until the outside of the cup is covered with fabric (except the drain hole). Spread the glue mixture over the fabric squares, too.
4. For a smooth upper rim, wrap some of the fabric squares over the rim and glue them to the inside of the cup. Let the flowerpots dry for a few days.

LARGE GROUP ACTIVITY: Rainbows

Getting Ready: Plant "rainbows." Prepare by buying mixed flower seeds: marigolds, zinnias, pansies, daisies, and asters. You will also need potting soil.

Directions:
1. Fill each flowerpot three-quarters full of soil.
2. Give each a pinch of seeds on top of the soil.
3. Cover the seeds with more planter mix, according to the directions on the packets.
4. Water and set the flowerpots on a sunny windowsill.
5. Keep the soil moist until the plants sprout and the rainbows bloom.

SHADOW BOX BOOK: Rr Page

(See directions on page 7.)

Picture-Word Suggestions—rose, rainbow, raccoon, rat, robin, reindeer, rocking horse, rake, railroad, ribbon, roof, ruler, raindrop, round, rocket

Name _____

Rainbow of Flowers

Directions: Color the flowers.

red tulip

orange poppy

yellow daisy

green fern

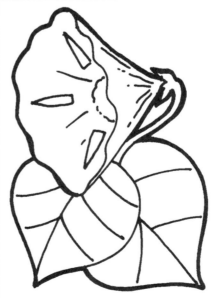

blue morning glory

purple pansy

Ring-a-Ring-a-Rosies

Directions: To play an action game with the rhyme, enlarge each R picture found below. Cut out and glue them onto small-sized paper plates. Place the plates on the floor in a circle. Have the children hold hands and form one large circle around the pictures, moving clockwise as they sing the rhyme. After they tumble down, the children pick up the nearest picture. Each child in turn then names their picture. After placing the pictures on the floor again, everyone stands up and the game continues.

> **RHYME:**
> **Ring-a-Ring-a-Rosies**
> Ring-a-ring-a-rosies,
> A pocketful of posies;
> Ashes, ashes,
> We all fall down!

rake	rainbow	rain	rope
ruler	ring	rock	reindeer
robin	raisins	raccoon	rabbit
ribbon	raspberries	road	rice

Rhyming Riddles

Getting Ready: Many generations of children have enjoyed rhyming riddles. Cut apart the riddle and picture cards on pages 100–102. Color the picture cards and then laminate them. Place the riddle cards in a stack. Arrange the picture cards on the chalkboard tray or attach them to a bulletin or felt board where everyone can see them.

> **RHYME: Riddle Me**
> Riddle me, riddle me, ree,
> A hawk sat upon the tree;
> And he says to himself, says he,
> "Oh dear, what a fine bird I be!"

Directions: Read each riddle aloud and have the children guess which picture is the answer.

There was a girl in our town,
Silk an' satin was her gown,
Silk an' satin, gold an' velvet,
Guess her name — three times I've
    said it.

(Ann)

Formed long ago, yet made today,
Employed while others sleep;
What few would like to give away,
Nor many wish to keep.

(bed)

Little Nanny Etticote
Has a white petticoat,
With a red nose;
The longer she stands,
The shorter she grows.

(candle)

Black within and red without;
Four corners round about.

(chimney)

Humpty Dumpty sat on a wall,
Humpty Dumpty had a great fall;
All the king's horses,
    and all the king's men,
Couldn't put Humpty Dumpty
    together again.

(egg)

I took a walk and chewed some gum.
I saw a store selling fingers and
    thumbs.

(gloves)

Riddle me, riddle me,
What is that
Over the head
and under the hat?

(hair)

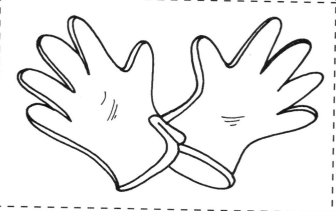

As I was going to St. Ives,
I met a man with seven wives.
Every wife had seven sacks;
Every sack had seven cats;
Every cat had seven kittens.
Kittens, cats, sacks, and wives,
How many were going to St. Ives?

(one)

Purple, yellow, red, and green,
The King cannot reach it,
    nor the Queen;
Nor can old Noll, whose power's
    so great.
Tell me the riddle while I count
    to eight.

(rainbow)

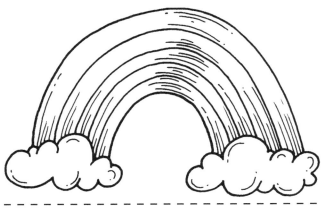

Higher than a house, higher than a tree,
Oh, whatever can it be?

(star)

Thirty white horses
Up on a red hill,
Now they tramp,
Now they champ,
Now they stand still.

(teeth and gums)

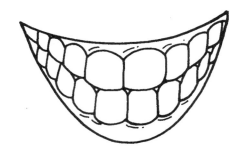

"S" Is for Seuss and Signing

CHILDREN'S BOOK: Dr. Seuss's ABC:
An Amazing Alphabet Book!
Written and illustrated by Dr. Seuss

This whimsical board book takes children into a wonderful world of zany writing and silly, colorful caricatures to help them learn the alphabet.

CIRCLE TIME: Alphabet Fun

After reading each page, encourage the children to think of two, three, or four other words that begin with the same letter. Use the new words to replace certain words in the book and reread each page.

Example: "Big Q, little q what begins with Q? The quick Queen of Quincy and her quacking quacker-oo." If children suggest: quiet, quilt, and quiz, you might read it like this: "Big Q, little q what begins with Q? The quizzing Queen of quilts and her quiet quacker-oo." The children will be amazed at how creative their new lines are. List the new text on the board for the following activity.

CRAFT: Classroom Big Book

Pass out large sheets of drawing paper. The children will choose one of the new lines from the board to illustrate. When the pictures have been drawn and colored, help the children write the appropriate lines beneath their pictures. Collate the pages into a classroom alphabet big book.

PHONICS: Letter Recognition

Getting Ready: If appropriate, reproduce the Manual Alphabet below for each child.

Directions: Explain to the children that deaf people often communicate with a manual alphabet called Sign Language. As you reread the book, have the children sign the appropriate letters. After signing the story, allow time for the children to learn how to sign the letters in their names.

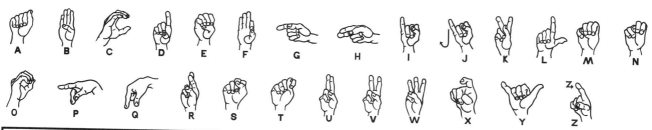

SHADOW BOX BOOK: Ss Page

(See directions on page 7.)

Picture-Words Suggestions—saw, sea, seal, six, seven, sky, sun, sand, sailboat, Saturn, seahorse, seagull, scissors

Sing a Song of Sixpence

<table>
<tr><td colspan="2">RHYME: Sing a Song of Sixpence</td></tr>
<tr>
<td>
Sing a song of sixpence,
A pocketful of rye;
Four-and-twenty blackbirds
Baked in a pie.
</td>
<td>
When the pie was opened,
The birds began to sing;
Wasn't that a dainty dish
To set before the king?
</td>
</tr>
</table>

Directions: Choose several children to be "blackbirds." These children will stand in the center. The rest of the children join hands and form a circle around the blackbirds. As the children sing the first line of the verse, they move in a circle counterclockwise. On the second line, the circle continues right and closes in on the blackbirds. As the children sing "When the pie was opened, . . ." the circle moves left and opens up. On the next line (Wasn't that . . ."), the blackbirds try to escape by breaking through the joined hands. The children whose hands release become the blackbirds in the next round.

Alternative: Have the children sing the song while sitting. When you get to the word "blackbirds" in the first verse, point to a child who fills in the blank with an S word. Example: "Four-and-twenty sand castles baked in a pie." In the second verse, replace the word "birds" with a new S word.

Silly Pies

Directions: Recite the rhyme "Sing a Song of Sixpence." Discuss the idea of blackbirds being in a pie. Ask the children, "What other silly things that begin with the letter S can be baked in a pie?"

On light-brown construction paper, reproduce the pie pattern found on page 105 for each child. Have the children draw or glue pictures of things that begin with the letter S on their pies—the sillier, the better! If needed, offer some examples: shoe pie, snail pie, smile pie, swan pie, snake pie, star pie, starfish pie, sunflower pie, skateboard pie, soccer ball pie, sun pie, skunk pie, and spider pie.

Sneeze on Monday

<table>
<tr><td colspan="2">RHYME: Sneeze</td></tr>
<tr>
<td>
Sneeze on Monday, sneeze for danger;
Sneeze on Tuesday, kiss a stranger;
Sneeze on Wednesday, receive a letter;
</td>
<td>
Sneeze on Thursday, something better;
Sneeze on Friday, expect sorrow;
Sneeze on Saturday, joy tomorrow.
</td>
</tr>
</table>

Directions: Practice singing the rhyme to the tune of "Twinkle, Twinkle, Little Star." When the children know the rhyme, replace the word "sneeze" with a pretend sneezing sound. Then sing the rhyme by replacing the sound of a sneeze with each of the following: snap, sniff, snore, and snort.

Alternative: Make the rhyme an action game. The leader names an action. The class sings the new rhyme while one child performs the action. Example: Skate on Monday, . . . (swim, strut, swing, surf, stumble, stroll, stoop, sweep, somersault, or sway.)

Name _____

Directions: Think of words that start with the /s/ sound. Find and cut out pictures that begin with the letter S and glue them on the pie.

Silly Pie Pattern

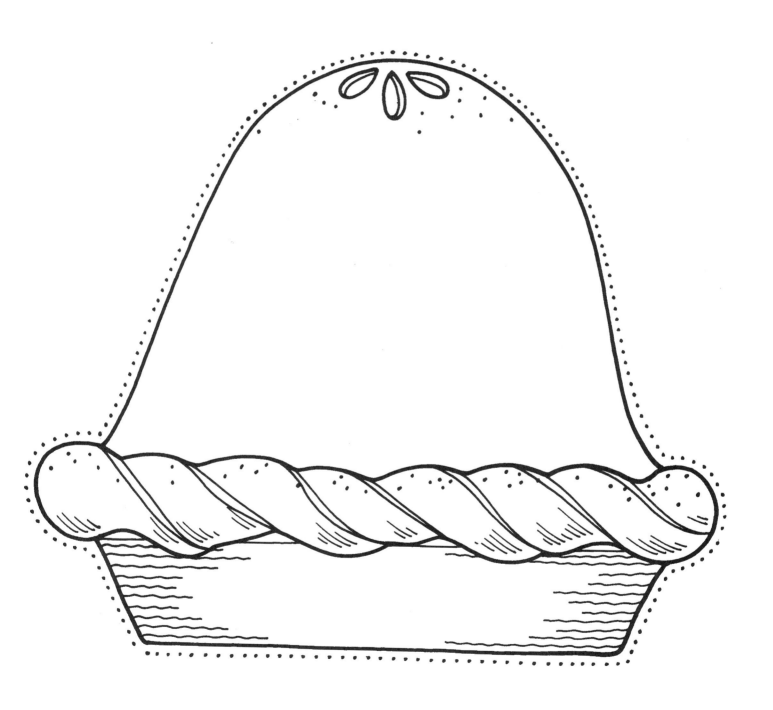

Swim or Soar?

Name _____

Directions: Cut out and color the animal stamps on page 107. Say the name of each animal. On this page, paste each stamp above or below the sea to show whether the animal flies or swims.

Swim or Soar? Patterns

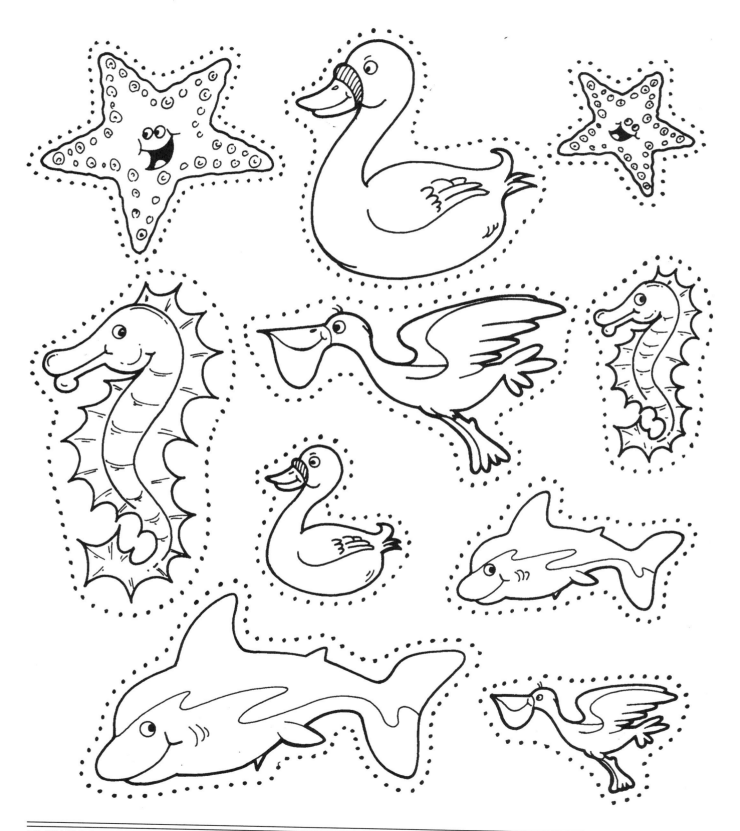

"T" Is for Toes and Tongue Twisters

Tt

turtle

CHILDREN'S BOOK: Busy Toes
Written by C. W. Bowie and
illustrated by Fred Willingham

Beautiful larger-than-life illustrations of dozens of things that toes can do like wave, tickle, draw, dig, splash, and squish will engage young readers. These images are a sweet reminder of just how wonderful toes can be. Toes come in all shapes and sizes—long and thin, short and fat, and the longest toe is not always the big toe. Have the children remove their shoes and socks before reading *Busy Toes*. Encourage everyone to wiggle their toes during the story.

As you read each page, ask who has used their toes to do each thing? Encourage the children to answer with a show of toes.

Examples:

- Has anyone ever tickled someone's toes?
- Have you ever rubbed your dog's tummy with your toes?
- Have you ever tried to draw or write with your toes?
- Have you ever buried your toes in hot sand?
- Have you ever used your toes to test the water temperature before getting into the bathtub?
- Have you ever walked barefoot through mud puddles? How did it feel?
- Have you ever walked barefoot in the rain? How did it feel?
- Can you walk on tiptoes? Let's try it.
- Have you ever seen a baby sucking her toes?
- Have you ever waved with your toes? Let's try it.

CRAFT: Toe Art

Using fine-tip water soluble pens, have the children draw a face on each of their toes. Afterwards, they can introduce their toe families to friends.

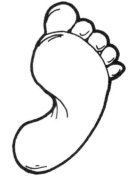

GAMES: Relay Games

Play some toe relay games. Try these toes-only stunts:
- Pick up a sock, put it in a bucket, and then run back to team.
- Push a plastic toy car across a room.
- Draw the letter T with a crayon.
- Pick up 10 marbles and drop them into a container.

PHONICS: Letter Recognition

Have the children use their feet to form the letter T. Try forming other lowercase letters: b, d, h, l, p, q, u, and v.

CHILDREN'S BOOK: Hello Toes! Hello Feet!
Written by Ann Whitford Paul and
illustrated by Nadine Bernard Westcott

This delightful book is written in rhyme. It is the story of a little girl's toes taking her through the day. The book is full of great sounds that the children can make.

As you read *Hello Toes! Hello Feet!* the children can make time-out signals with their hands each time they hear a word that begins with a /t/ sound. Examples in the book include toes, tangled, touch, table, try, touch, trot, to, trees, and time.

LARGE GROUP ACTIVITY: Reread

Reread the book. This time stop at words that end with the letter T. Children might indicate if the /t/ sound is heard by holding up their feet.

Examples: feet, first, closet, let, eat, point, get, trot, fast, first, last

LARGE GROUP ACTIVITY: Tongue Twisters

Give the children an opportunity to speak in five- to six-word sentences and also reinforce the /t/ sound with these tongue twisters based on nursery rhymes. Recite and then let the children try.

- Tip, top, tower, tumbled down in town.
- Tiny Tommy Tucker sings for his supper.
- Hub-a-dub, dub; three men scrubbed a tub.
- Tweedle-dum and Tweedle-dee went to town for tea.
- To town, to town, to buy a fat bun; home again, home again, shopping is done.
- To market, to market, a gallop, a trot, to buy some meat to put in the pot.
- Twiddlum, twaddlum, twenty-two, T-w-o spells two.
- Trip and go, heave and ho! Up and down, to and fro.

SHADOW BOX BOOK: Tt Page

(See directions on page 7.)

Picture-Word Suggestions—table, tan, ten, teddy bear, tadpole, toad, toucan, tiger, turkey, turtle, toe, top, toy, TV, tail, tooth, tomato

Sing "Twinkle, Twinkle, Little Star"

RHYME: Twinkle, Twinkle, Little Star

Twinkle, twinkle, little star,
How I wonder what you are!
Up above the world so high,
Like a diamond in the sky.

When the blazing sun is gone,
When the nothing shines upon,
Then you show your little light,
Twinkle, twinkle, all the night.

When the traveler in the dark
Thanks you for your tiny spark;
How could he see where to go
If you did not twinkle so?

In the dark blue sky you keep,
Often through my curtains peep,
For you never shut your eye,
Till the sun is in the sky.

As your bright and tiny spark
Lights the traveler in the dark,
Though I know not what you are,
Twinkle, twinkle, little star.

Directions: The tune for "Twinkle, Twinkle, Little Star" is actually an old French melody. It is one of the most familiar tunes and it is often used to sing the "Alphabet Song" (see page 142) and "Baa, Baa, Black Sheep" (see page 16). Hum the tune with the children to make sure they are familiar with it. Most people know the first verse, but very few have ever heard or sung the other verses. At the end of each verse, repeat these two lines as the chorus: "Twinkle, twinkle, little star, How I wonder what you are!"

Thirty Days Has September

Directions: Practice the rhyme with your children. If the last two lines are too difficult for the children to learn, end the rhyme after the fourth line and change the last words like this:
Thirty days has September,
April, June, and November;
All the rest have thirty-one,
Except February which has twenty-eight.

**RHYME:
Thirty Days Has September**
Thirty days has September,
April, June, and November;
All the rest have thirty-one,
Except February, alone,
And that has twenty-eight days clear
And twenty-nine in each leap year.

If this rhyme about the number of days in each month is too advanced for your group, play another game such as tiddledywinks, tug-of-war, tag, or tossing a ball. There are tons of terrific things to teach that begin with the letter T.

Tom, Tom, the Piper's Son

Directions: Use the verses of "Tom, Tom, the Piper's Son" to make a four-page book. Copy and cut out the pages provided. The children will illustrate each verse, color the pictures, and staple the pages together in book form.

Tom, Tom, the piper's son,
He learned to play when he was young;
But all the tune that he could play
Was "Over the hills and far away."

Now, Tom with his pipe made such a noise,
That he pleased both the girls and the boys.
And they all stopped to hear him play,
"Over the hills and far away."

Tom, Tom, the Piper's Son

Book Cover Directions: Children may want to make and decorate construction paper covers for their booklets. Help them print the title of the rhyme on the front cover of their books. Staple the pages together along the left edge of each booklet.

Tom with his pipe did play with such skill,
That those who heard him could never stand still;
Whenever they heard him they began to dance.
Even pigs on their hind legs would after him prance.

He met Old Dame Trot with a basket of eggs,
He used his pipe and she used her legs.
She danced about till her eggs were all broke;
She began to fret, but he laughed at the joke.

Tic-Tac-Toe "T's"

Name _____

Directions: Draw or cut and paste pictures that match the words in three spaces to make a straight line down, across, or diagonally.

tiger	television	toes
toast	turtle	toy
table	tent	ten

"U" Is for Unicorns and Underwear

Uu

umbrella

CHILDREN'S BOOK:
Unicorns! Unicorns!
Written by Geraldine McCaughrean
and illustrated by Sophie Windham

This story is a legend about the extinction of unicorns. On their way to the ark that Noah built, the unicorns stopped several times to help other animals, causing them to miss boarding the boat.

After reading the story once without pausing for discussion, reread it. This time have the children find animals in the pictures. Discuss the initial sound of each animal name.

GAME: Listening

Play a listening game. Name a pair of animals. The children can indicate if the animal names rhyme by nodding or shaking their heads.

- cat, rat
- buffalo, mosquito
- flamingo, tiger
- rhino, hippo
- fly, bee
- iguana, panda
- badger, tiger
- kiwi, hyenas
- dog, hog
- eagle, beagle
- swallow, crow
- zebra, gorilla
- piranha, cheetah
- worm, spider
- boa, cobra
- collie, donkey

CHILDREN'S BOOK: Arthur's Underwear
Written and illustrated by Marc Brown

This title is the author's twenty-fifth Arthur Adventure book. To avoid the nightmare of going to school in his underwear, Arthur tries all kinds of tricks including not falling asleep.

Share the story about Arthur having nightmares that he will forget to put on his pants before going to school. When his worst nightmare finally comes true—Arthur finds himself at school without pants—he learns that it is not the end of the world. Follow up with a discussion about nightmares. You will need plenty of time to hear everyone's story. Kids love to talk about their dreams.

Riddle:
"What are you wearing under there?"
"Under where?"
"Oh, underwear."

SHADOW BOX BOOK: Uu Page   (See directions on page 7.)
Picture-Words Suggestions—(short vowel sound) umbrella, undershirt, upside-down cake; (long vowel sound) ukulele, unicycle, unicorn

---

Upon My Word

RHYME: Upon My Word

Upon my word and honor,
As I went to Bonner,
I met a pig
Without a wig,
Upon my word and honor.

Directions: Recite the rhyme several times until the class knows it by heart. Then talk about the rhyme pattern. The last words in the first, second, and fifth lines rhyme. The last words in the third and fourth lines rhyme. The idea of a pig in a wig is fun and interesting. What unique animal rhyme combinations can the class invent to create new jingles? Give the children some examples, and then let them make up some of their own. Say the rhyme with each new rhyming word pair.

Upon my word and honor,
As I went to Bonner,
I met a cat
Without a hat,
Upon my word and honor.

Examples:

cat, hat
frog, log
bird, word
mouse, house
toad, road
ants, pants
bee, knee
fish, dish
antelope, cantaloupe
llama, mama
kangaroo, kazoo

Learning ABC's Through Literature and Rhymes

Name _____

Unbelievable "U's"

RHYME: Up by the Chimney
Up by the chimney there is a small man,
Who holds in his hands a stick and a fan;
When the winds rage he strikes a fierce blow,
And thus their direction tells mortals below.

Directions: Many "U's" are hidden in the picture below. Can you find them? Trace each letter U with your favorite color crayon.

Uniquely Me

RHYME: "U" Is a Unicorn
"U" is a unicorn
Who, as it said,
Wears an ivory bodkin
On his forehead.

Getting Ready: One thing that makes a unicorn unique is its horn. What makes each child unique? Encourage the children to think about those things that make them different from all others.

Directions: When the class is outside, have the children form a large circle. Place a ball in front of one child's feet. The child recites a new version of the rhyme listed below.

Example: "The letter U is unique, and I _____."
(*She fills in the blank with something special about herself, such as "have red hair."*)

Then she gently kicks the ball across the circle to another child who stops it with his feet. That child says, "The letter U is unique, and I _____." (*He fills in the blank about himself this time.*) Continue until all the children have had a turn.

Discussion: Remind the children that there are many ways for us to be unique. Every single person is unique, even twins are not exactly alike. Being different makes us special and beautiful.

Variation: After the discussion, you may want to review some of the things the children said about themselves. Examples: "Who said that he collects baseball cards? What did Rosa say was her favorite color?" Let the children name things that they find unique about each other. Stress that the statements should be positive and always kind. You may choose to write each child's name on the chalkboard and list the things the children say about each other.

"U" Is Uniquely You

Directions: As the children study the letter U, explain the definition of unique. Then celebrate their uniqueness by making paper dolls. Begin by folding and cutting out paper dolls for each child. See the step-by-step directions and the patterns below. As the children unfold the dolls, explain that each of the dolls is alike, a carbon copy of the next one. People are not like that. Each person is a unique and special human unlike all others. Discuss with the children the things that make each one of them special. Then have the children decorate each doll in a different way.

1. Fold the paper once.   2. Fold again.   3. Fold one more time.   4. Place the pattern on the fold and cut it out.

 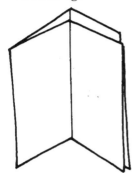 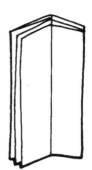 

5. Unfold the paper.   6. Color and decorate each doll to make it unique.

"U" Is Uniquely You Patterns

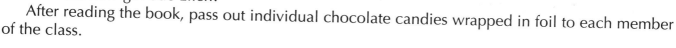

"V"
Is for Valentines

CHILDREN'S BOOK:
Arthur's Valentine
Written and illustrated
by Marc Brown

Who is Arthur's secret admirer? The children will enjoy this mystery as they work on the letter V. Before reading the story, take a vote. Is Arthur's secret admirer:

- his friend Fern?
- his best friend Buster playing a joke?
- Francine who has a crush on him and likes to tease him?
- or the new girl Sue Ellen?

After reading the book, pass out individual chocolate candies wrapped in foil to each member of the class.

CRAFT: Make Valentines

After pointing out that the bottom half of a valentine shape resembles the letter V, have the children make valentines. Demonstrate how to fold a piece of paper and cut half of the shape of a heart. For those children who cannot do this, create some patterns that they can use to outline their valentine shapes before cutting. See the patterns on page 120 for a variety of sizes. Provide craft materials for decorating the valentines, such as lace, stickers, foil stars, buttons, bows, and glitter.

CRAFT: Poster Hearts

To make a poster heart, have each child cut out one large pink heart. Using red poster paint, have the children make a handprint in the center of their heart shape. When the paint is dry, help the children write messages on their very special valentines.

BONUS FUN: Arthur's Fan Club

Arthur has a fan club and a reading association. Your children who can read may want to join. Information can be found on the back cover of Arthur books.

SHADOW BOX BOOK: Vv Page

(See directions on page 7.)

Picture-Word Suggestions—violin, van, vegetables, violets, vulture, valentine, vines, vowels, vampire

---

Valentine Patterns

Very Important Names

Directions: As you recite the rhyme below, direct the children to listen for the rhyming words. Then as a class create a new rhyme. Have each child say the first letter of her name and a phrase describing herself. Record each statement on a card. When finished, alphabetize the cards and read the class rhyme aloud.

A is Ann, carrying milk from the cow.

B is Benjamin, taking a bow.

C is Charlotte, gathering flowers.

D is Dick, one of the mowers.

E is Eliza, feeding a hen.

F is Frank, mending his pen.

G is Georgiana, shooting an arrow.

H is Harry, wheeling a barrow.

I is Isabella, gathering fruit.

J is John, playing the flute.

K is Katie, nursing her dolly.

L is Lawrence, feeding poor Polly.

M is Maria, learning to draw.

N is Nicholas, without a flaw.

O is Octavius, riding a goat.

P is Penelope, sailing a boat.

Q is Quintus, holding a lance.

R is Rachel, learning to dance.

S is Sarah, talking to the cook.

T is Tommy, reading a book.

U is Urban, rolling the green.

V is Victoria, eating a bean.

W is Walter, flying a kite.

X is Xerxes, a boy of great might.

Y is Yolanda, eating bread.

Z is Zachariah, going to bed.

Best Vest in the West

Finally, have the children decorate their vests with the V things below. Decorate the patterns with cutouts, sequins, ribbon, rickrack, yarn, and markers.

Directions: You will need one brown-paper grocery bag for each child. Turn it upside down. Cut out openings for the neck and arms as shown below.

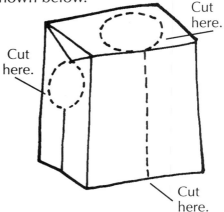

Cut the bottom of the vest (see suggestions below) to make a decorative edge or leave it plain.

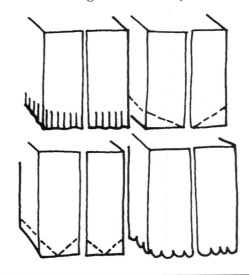

Learning ABC's Through Literature and Rhymes

See the "V's"?

Name _____

Directions: Look for things in the picture that start with the letter V. Can you see the vulture? What other V things can you find? Look closely and you will see a vine, volcano, valley, vest, vase, violets, and a violin. Color the V things.

RHYME: "V" Is for Vulture
"V" is a vulture
That eats a great deal.

"W" Is for Wild Things and Wolves

CHILDREN'S BOOK:
Where the Wild Things Are
Written and illustrated
by Maurice Sendak

Ww

wolf

This book is a classic. After the children have had an opportunity to hear this delightful story without any interruptions, reread the story aloud. This time, have the children participate by adding sound effects or answering questions. For example:

- What kind of mischief do you think Max made?
- Max's mother called him "Wild Thing." What wild things do you do?
- The wild things roared their terrible roars. How do you think that sounded?
- The wild things rolled their terrible eyes. Show me what you think they did.
- The wild things showed their terrible claws. Show me your terrible claws.
- All together, roll your eyes, show your claws, and roar your terrible roar. Go!

GAME: Pick a Max

Find out who can stare the longest. Pair children and have them stare at each other until one child blinks. Round-robin fashion, repeat the game until you have a class staring champ. Crown that child "Max of the Class"!

CRAFT: Making Masks

To make "Wild Thing" masks, cut eye holes in paper plates and then decorate them with markers and other craft materials. Attach craft-stick handles so the masks may be held by the children in front of their faces while dramatizing the story.

CHILDREN'S BOOK:

Pedro the Brave
Written by Leo Broadley and illustrated by Holly Swain

This book is written in rhyme. It is about a very courageous and smart boy, his dog Dusty, Ronnie the horse, and a very gullible wolf.

Without pausing for discussion, read aloud the book *Pedro the Brave*. If interested, reread it and have the children identify rhyming words. Make a list on the board. Rhyming words in the book include the following examples:

- curly—early
- red—said
- hot—pot
- ham—jam
- toes—nose
- bed—said
- stars—guitars
- behave—brave
- diet—try it
- head—instead

CRAFT: Hot Sauce

Reread the recipe for Pedro's hot sauce. Then have children use red, yellow, and orange crayons to draw a picture of the wolf after tasting the hot sauce.

CHILDREN'S BOOK: Wolf
Written by Becky Bloom and illustrated by Pascal Biet

This book is about animals who can read. Children who are learning to read will especially enjoy the story of a duck, pig, and cow who calm a wolf by educating him.

Read the story aloud. Have the children listen for the "hw" sound at the beginning of words. Using three fingers to form a "W," have the children signal every time they hear the initial /w/ sound.

DRAMATIZATION: Wolf

Encourage careful listening by having the children turn one of the wolf books, *Pedro the Brave* or *Wolf* (or even the *Three Little Pigs*) into a skit. Reread both books and then break the children into groups of four. If dramatizing *Pedro the Brave*, the characters will be Pedro, Dusty, Ronnie, and the wolf. If dramatizing *Wolf*, the players are wolf, pig, cow, and duck. Encourage the children to turn their skits into musicals with the song that follows. Allow plenty of time for the children to rehearse the skits. After practicing, share the skits in a large group.

SONG: Wolves

(Sing to the tune of "Who's Afraid of the Big Bad Wolf?")

Wolves:
Who's afraid of the big, bad wolf?
The big bad wolf. The big bad wolf.
Who's afraid of the big, bad wolf?
Aaa OOOOO ooo ooo ooo ooo!

Pig:
I'm not afraid of the big, bad wolf.
The big bad wolf. The big bad wolf.
I'm not afraid of the big, bad wolf.
Oink, oink, oink, oink, oink!

Duck:
I'm not afraid of the big, bad wolf.
The big bad wolf. The big bad wolf.
I'm not afraid of the big, bad wolf.
Quack, quack, quack, quack, quack!

Cow:
I'm not afraid of the big, bad wolf.
The big bad wolf. The big bad wolf.
I'm not afraid of the big, bad wolf.
Moo, moo, moo, moo, moo!

Pedro:
I'm not afraid of the big, bad wolf.
The big bad wolf. The big bad wolf.
I'm not afraid of the big, bad wolf.
Tra, la, la, la, la!

Dusty the dog:
I'm not afraid of the big, bad wolf.
The big bad wolf. The big bad wolf.
I'm not afraid of the big, bad wolf.
Bowwow, bowwow-wow

Ronnie the horse:
I'm not afraid of the big, bad wolf.
The big bad wolf. The big bad wolf.
I'm not afraid of the big, bad wolf.
Neigh, neigh, neigh, neigh, neigh.

SHADOW BOX BOOK: Ww Page

(See directions on page 7.)

Picture-Word Suggestions—wagon, water, wax, white, wolf, weasel, woodpecker, walrus, wasp, worm, watermelon, web, wood, windmill, wall

Whistle, Whistle, Whistle

RHYME: Whistle, Whistle
Whistle, daughter, whistle; whistle, daughter, dear.
I cannot whistle, Mammy; I cannot whistle clear.
Whistle, daughter, whistle; whistle for a pound.
I cannot whistle, Mammy; I cannot make a sound.

Directions: Some children can whistle and some cannot. One way to whistle is to make a small O shape with the lips. Place the tongue behind the lower front teeth, and as you tighten the lips, force air out between them. Share this method of whistling and let the children practice. Then invite others to demonstrate how they whistle. Make a list of steps for different ways to whistle. Have the children experiment by whistling in these different ways. Once everyone can whistle in one way or another, divide the group into two parts. One group whistles while the other group says the rhyme. Then switch roles, and let the first group that whistled say the rhyme as the second group now whistles.

Play a whistling guessing game. Let the children take turns whistling familiar tunes while the others guess the name of the tune.

Alternative: While everyone is sitting in a circle, have one child leave the room. While she is out, point to someone who will be the official whistler. When the child returns to the class, everyone pretends to whistle while only the official whistler really whistles. The person who left the room tries to guess who is whistling. When she guesses correctly, she gets to choose someone to leave the room and the game is repeated.

Find Out: What is the longest song that can be whistled without stopping to take in air? Who can whistle on the in-breath as well as the out-breath? Who can whistle the loudest? Softest? Where do we hear whistles? (on the playground, at sporting events, train stations, and factories.)

Watermelon Wishes

RHYME: Three Good Wishes
Three good wishes, three good kisses,
I will give to thee.

Directions: Discuss the meaning of wishes, and let the children share what they would request if their wishes could come true. Reproduce the watermelon pattern onto red construction paper for each child. Have each child record three wishes on the watermelon and then color the rind green and the seeds black. Alternatively, attach real watermelon seeds to the worksheets. When everyone has completed the activity, assemble the pages into a class book. To reinforce the pages, laminate them or cover each one with clear self-adhesive plastic before assembling the book. Place the book where members of the class can read it in their spare time.

Alternative:

Use the watermelon worksheets to border a bulletin board or room.

Hang the watermelon slices from a coat hanger to make a class mobile.

Watermelon Wishes Pattern

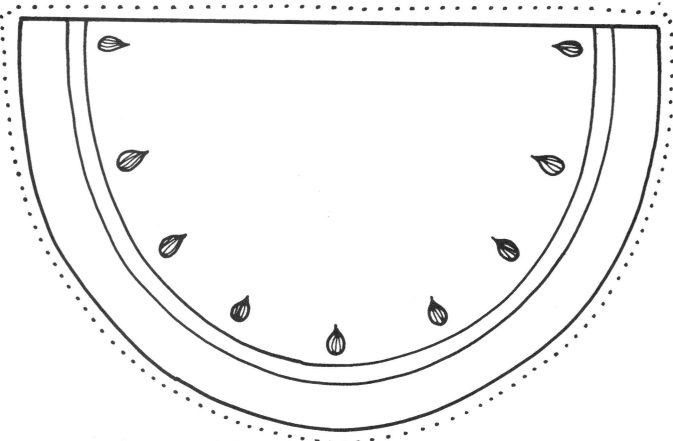

Wee Willie Winkie

Getting Ready: To play this game, the children need to have memorized the rhyme. It is best to play this game outside if the air is warm and the ground is dry.

Directions: Someone is chosen to be Wee Willie Winkie. Everyone else finds a spot that is his "home." While chanting the rhyme, the players leave their homes and run around. When the last line of the rhyme is spoken, everyone should scramble back to their original spot and lie down. Anyone caught still wandering around after ten o'clock is chased by Wee Willie Winkie who tries to tag him. If a person is tagged, that person will be Wee Willie Winkie in the next round.

RHYME: Wee Willie Winkie
Wee Willie Winkie
Runs through the town,
Upstairs and downstairs,
In his nightgown;

Rapping at the window,
Crying at the lock,
"Are the children in their beds,
For now it's ten o'clock?"

Variations: After the children have played the game by running, replace the word "runs" in the rhyme with walks, waltzes, or wobbles. Children should chant or move in the appropriate way. Examples: everyone whines, whispers, or whistles the chant, as they walk, waltz, or wobble through the town. See if anyone can think of yet another W word as an alternative for the chant and game.

Wee Willie Winkie

Name _____

Directions: Can you see Wee Willie Winkie running through the town? What other things that begin with the letter W can you see? Hidden in the picture are a waffle, watch, worm, wagon, walrus, weasel, whale, woodpecker, walnut, and web. Color Wee Willie Winkie and the W things you find in the picture.

"X"
Is for Xylophone

Children's Book: The Jungle ABC
Written and illustrated
by Michael Roberts

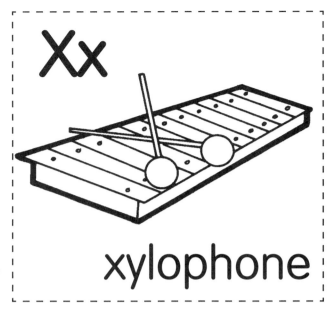

Xx

xylophone

This is a wordless book that will turn reviewing the letters A–Z into a mysterious journey. Each exotic picture suggests an African object.

Introduce *The Jungle ABC* with the page for the letter X. See if anyone can figure out what musical instrument it is. Then flip back to the beginning of the book, and as you show each page, have the children take turns tracing the featured letter with an index finger.

After identifying the letter, encourage the children to try to name each object suggested by the picture. When necessary, use a question or statement as a prompt.

A – Do you see the head of a horned animal? (antelope)
B – Do you see a whole bunch of fruit? (bananas)
C – What do you call a lizard that can change colors? (chameleon)
D – Can you name the musical instruments? (drums)
E – What animal has a long trunk? (elephant)
F – What are they dancing around? (fire)
G – What partially shown animal do you see? (giraffe)
H – What kind of water-dwelling animal do you see? (hippopotamus)
I – Do you see a herd of loping animals? Name them. (impalas)
J – The secret word for this page is not a person or thing; it is a place. (jungle)
K – This may be a new word for you; it means an African village. (kraal)
L – This large cat does not have stripes; it has spots. (leopard)
M – This is something that might be worn on the face. (mask)
N – This is not the animals shown; it's a time of day. (night)
O – These flowers are rare and beautiful. (orchids)
P – Some kinds of these birds can talk. (parrots)
Q – This woman might be married to the king. (queen)
R – The men are running from a horned animal. (rhinoceros)
S – What do you see slithering in the grass? (snakes) How many?
T – What is a group of men and women who live together called? (tribe)
U – What are the men using to keep off the spray? (umbrellas)
V – Some women can perfectly balance these objects on their heads. (vases)
W – This animal may be new to you. Its name sounds a bit like "wild beast." (wildebeests)
X – This is certainly a different kind of musical instrument. You have probably seen it m a d e of metal, not bones. (xylophone)
Y – This yummy, yellow treat tastes very much like sweet potatoes. (yams)
Z – These striped animals are not zebus. What are they? (zebras)

GAME: Here We Go 'Round the Alphabet

To review the letters, write each lowercase letter on a large sheet of paper. In random order, stack the letters and place them on the floor. Holding hands and using the tune of "Here We Go 'Round the Mulberry Bush," have the children sing as they circle the letter.

Here we go 'round the alphabet,
The alphabet, the alphabet.
Here we go 'round the alphabet,
We're learning a to z.

Point to a child (matching the first name to a letter when possible) to move into the circle and hold up the top letter. Everyone then walks around her and sings the new verse.

(Name of child) is holding the letter b.
The letter b, the letter b.
(Name of child) is holding the letter b.
We're learning a to z.

Then the child hands the letter to you and joins the circle. Repeat until all the letters have been featured and everyone has had a turn standing inside the circle. On another occasion, use the uppercase letters to play the game.

RECIPE: Bake Alphabet Cookies

Bake alphabet cookies using commercially prepared refrigerator cookie dough. Begin by assigning the children specific letters. To make a cookie, give each child about four large spoonfuls of dough. Working on waxed paper, the child shapes the dough into a ball, rolls it into a rope, and forms the letter. Roll the cookie in sugar and bake it on a baking sheet as indicated on the package. When the cookies are baked, have each child hold up his cookie and say the letter name.

SHADOW BOX BOOK: Xx Page
Picture-Word Suggestions—x-ray, x-ray fish, taxi, fox, box

(See directions on page 7.)

"X" Was King Xerxes

RHYME:
"X" Was King Xerxes
"X" was King Xerxes,
Who, if you don't know,
Reigned over Persia
A great while ago.

Directions: Use the pattern below to make an extra-special stand-up king. Color and decorate the king's crown and robe with bright colors and glitter. Cut out the king and glue the picture around a toilet tissue cardboard tube so that the king can stand.

Name _____

Animal X-Rays

Directions: Draw a line connecting each animal with the picture that looks most like its X ray. Color the animals.

Nixie, Dixie

Name _____

Directions: Draw a line of twine to connect the 13 Dutchmen.

RHYME: Nixie, Dixie
Nixie, dixie, hickory bow,
Thirteen Dutchmen in a row;
Two corporals hold
A piece of twine,
To help the
Dutchmen form a line.

"Y"
Is for Yaks

CHILDREN'S BOOK: Animalia
Written and illustrated
by Graeme Base

This is a different kind of alphabet book. Its pages are filled with both familiar and exotic things. There is a wealth of hidden objects and ideas that turn each picture into a mystery.

Show the letter Y page first and discuss the sound it makes when saying the Y words. Read the pages randomly throughout the book, letting the children name the first sound of certain words.

SONG: Animalia

Begin on the first page of *Animalia* and as you turn the pages, use the tune of "Here We Go 'Round the Mulberry Bush" to sing the questions. Then have the children answer in tune.

Teacher Sings:
What armored animal begins with "A"?
Begins with "A"? Begins with "A"?
What armored animal begins with "A"?
Tell me if you can, please.

Children Sing:
An armored animal that begins with "A"?
Begins with "A," Begins with "A,"
Easy! It's armadillo.

Questions to Sing:
What armored animal begins with "A"? (armadillo)
What fluttering thing begins with "B"? (butterfly)
What colorful feline begins with "C"? (crimson cat)
What fire-breathing thing begins with "D"? (dragon)
What trumpeting animal begins with "E"? (elephant)
What croaking animal begins with "F"? (frog)
What hairy primate begins with "G"? (gorillas)
What harnessed beast begins with "H"? (horse)
What kind of lizard begins with "I"? (iguana)
What fox-like thing begins with "J"? (jackal)
What jumping animal begins with "K"? (kangaroo)
What roaring beast begins with "L"? (lion)
What squeaking animal begins with "M"? (mouse)
What salamander begins with "N"? (newt)
What long-legged bird begins with "O"? (ostrich)
What strutting bird begins with "P"? (peacock)

What speckled bird begins with "Q"? (quail)
What huge, horned beast begins with "R"? (rhinoceros)
What slithering animal begins with "S"? (snake)
What striped cat begins with "T"? (tiger)
What make-believe animal begins with "U"? (unicorn)
What road-kill eater begins with "V"? (vulture)
What flying insect begins with "W"? (wasp)
What bushy-tailed animal has "X" at the end? (fox)
What hairy, horned animal begins with "Y"? (yak)
What black-and-white animal begins with "Z"? (zebra)

LEARNING CENTER: Find the Hidden Pictures

Challenge the children to find hidden objects in the book. The author, Graeme Base, as a boy is hidden in every picture. Dressed in a yellow-and-orange striped sweater, on some pages he is easy to spot on some pages, while on others he is not. Each day, say the name of a new object for the children to find. If the child knows the first letter of the object, she can quickly find the picture on the correct page.

A – arches, abacus, ant, ambulance, alarm, acrobats, apple, airplane
B – bee, beetle, baboon, bonnet, bike, bed, bell, bull, bear
C – castle, cake, candle, cup, crab, can, clarinet, claws, cobra, camel, cap
D – doll, dominoes, dictionary, dragonfly, dog, dolphin, dart, door
E – eggs, exit, entry, eyes, eyeglasses
F – flowers, fire, fly, fox, fish, flamingo, fishing poles, finch, fin
G – grapes, gong, guitar, grasshopper, gopher, golf ball, giraffe
H – hammer, house, hyena, handkerchief, horn, hamsters, hummingbird
I – ink, icicle, iron, ice cream
J – joker, jack-in-the-box, judge, jug, jewelry, jaguar, jukebox, jam
K – kiwi, kettle, keys, knight, knife, kilt, King Kong
L – Lassie, leopard, lizard, lamb, lily, lamp, llama, lettuce, lute
M – microphone, medal, monster, map, moose, macaw, monkey, mask
N – newspaper, Neptune, Noah, note, net, nest, nurse, narwhal
O – oil, ox, owl, ocean, octagon, otter, oven, orange, octopus
P – package, Pope, panda, pumpkin, panda, parade, penguin, poodle, pears
Q – quart, quiver, quill, quail, queen, question marks
R – rose, rocking horse, rocking chair, raspberry, raccoon, rooster, ram, rocket
S – soccer ball, starfish, snail, Superman, scooter, spoon, Saturn, Santa
T – turtle, tricycle, telephone, toucan, top hat, target, tepee, tuba
U – umbrella, ukulele, Union Jack, Uncle Sam, university
V – vacuum, van, valentine, vegetable, vase, vine, vest
W– washing machine, wash, wishing well, wolf, wizard, whale, wall
X – X-mas tree, XXX = kiss in signature, x-ray, sign language for "X"
Y – yogurt, yolk, yoke, yawn, yeti, yeoman
Z – zoo, zoom, zap, zebu, zodiac

SHADOW BOX BOOK: Yy Page   (See directions on page 7.)
Picture-Word Suggestions—yarn, yam, yak, yawn, yolk, yellow, yacht

"Y" Is for Yodel

Directions: Demonstrate a yodel for the children. Explain that yodeling is a sudden change from chest voice to head voice. Recite the rhyme. When the children are familiar with the text, yodel the first three words of each verse instead of saying them. There is no right or wrong way to yodel, just have fun with it. Can someone yodel the last word in each of the last three lines of the verses?

Yodel "Yankee Doodle," too.

Yankee Doodle went to town
Riding on a pony;
He stuck a feather in his hat,
And called it Macaroni.

RHYME: Yaup, Yaup, Yaup
"Yaup, yaup, yaup!"
Said the croaking voice of a Frog.
"A rainy day
In the month of May,
And plenty of room in the bog."

"Yaup, yaup, yaup!"
Said the Frog: "It is charming weather.
We'll come and sup,
When the moon is up
And we'll all croak together."

Yaup, Yaup, Yaup!

Getting Ready: Say the rhyme. Ask the children if "yaup, yaup, yaup" is the sound they are used to hearing a frog make. What sound does a frog make? Have someone demonstrate the croaking of a frog. Let anyone who wants to croak like a frog have the opportunity. Then introduce an animal-voices guessing game.

Directions:
1. The first player repeats a sound three times he thinks a certain animal makes.
2. Then he points to someone who replies, "Said the voice of the (*name of animal*)."
3. If that person guesses the animal correctly, she provides the next clue. If she is incorrect, the first player repeats the sound and then points to another child.
4. The game continues until everyone has had the opportunity to make animal voices. Encourage creative animal sounds.

Yankee Doodle Hat

Directions: Reproduce the hat and feather patterns below on construction paper. Cut a strip of construction paper, long enough to wrap around a child's head. Staple the strip of paper to the hat so the child can enjoy wearing it while reciting the rhyme.

RHYME: Yankee Doodle
Yankee Doodle went to town
Riding on a pony;
He stuck a feather in his hat,
And called it Macaroni.

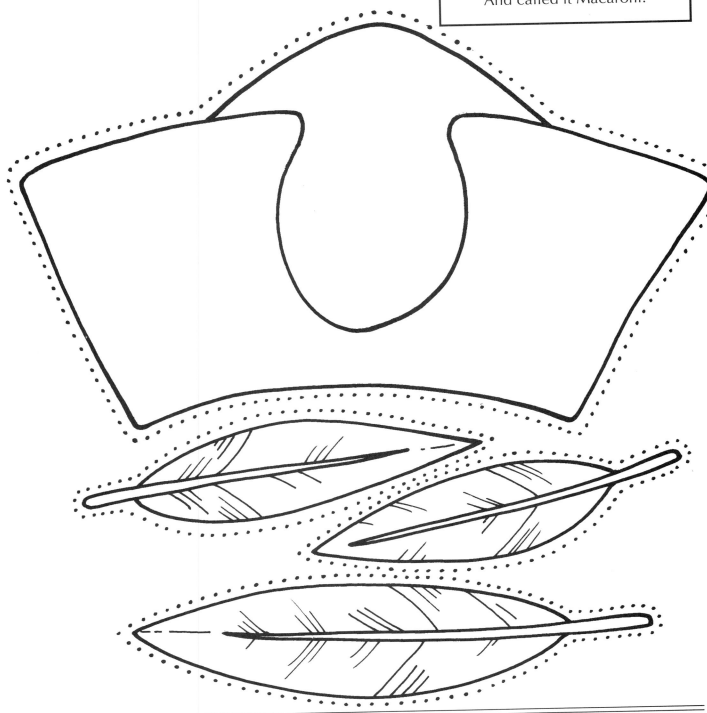

"Z"
Is for Zoom

Zz

zebra

CHILDREN'S BOOK: Alphabeep
Written by Debora Pearson

Zipping, zooming down the street—"A" is for ambulance; "B" is for bulldozer; all the way to "Z" for Zamboni®! Boys especially will enjoy this ABC parade on wheels. The cars, trucks, and machinery illustrated in vibrant primary colors provides great amusement.

CIRCLE TIME: Seasonal Clues

As you read and introduce each piece of machinery, ask the children to name the season. Look for clues like the weather and clothing.

GAME: Reread the Story

Pause to have the children make appropriate sounds for the machinery as you reread the book *Alphabeep*. Here are some examples:

- Ambulance—siren
- Bulldozer—clearing rubble
- Cement mixer—mixer turning, wet cement gushing out of a chute
- Dump truck—clatter, crash, ka-boom, dumping rocks
- Forklift—steel fingers of a forklift scraping the ground under heavy boxes
- Garbage truck—truck squishing the garbage
- Hook-and-ladder truck—fire truck siren, water rushing through a hose
- Ice-cream truck—tune of the ice cream truck
- Jeep®—sound of a horn, splashing through a stream, grinding up a steep hill
- Logging truck—truck changing gears as it roars down the road
- Moving truck—beep like a backing up truck
- Newspaper truck—sound of closing a metal door
- Police car—howl like a police siren, imitate a police radio
- Quarry excavator—gnawing apart rubble, dropping boulders
- Railroad crossing sign—sound of crossing bell; chug, chug of the train
- Street cleaner—swishing of brushes scrubbing the street
- Tow truck—truck hooking, reeling, and then dragging a car
- Utility truck—utility truck hoisting a worker up in its bucket
- Van—engine sounds, vehicle backing up
- Wrecking crane—iron ball swinging into the side of a building
- Zamboni®—sound of shaving ice heard where the machine works

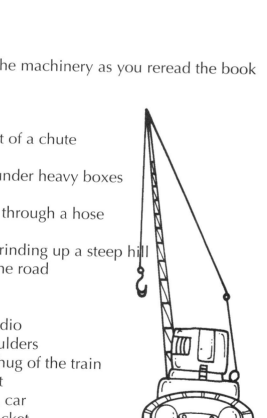

SHADOW BOX BOOK: Zz Page
Picture-Word Suggestions—zipper, zero, zebra, zoo, zinnias, zucchini

(See directions on page 7.)

"Z" Is a Zebra

RHYME: "Z" Is a Zebra
"Z" is a zebra,
That you've
Heard of before;
So here ends my rhyme
Till I find you some more.

Hairy, Green Zebra

Directions: To make a hairy, green zebra to celebrate the letter Z, provide each child with the following materials: a copy of the pattern below, a polystyrene foam cup, potting soil, and grass seed. Fill each cup nearly full of potting soil. Sprinkle grass seed on the soil. Lightly cover the seeds with soil. Use a green crayon to color some of the zebra's stripes. Cut out the zebra and glue it to the cup. Place the cup in a sunny spot and water enough to keep the soil moist. In about 10 days, the green zebra will have "hair."

"Z" Is for Zucchini

Although zucchini is a very versatile and delicious food, you may find that many of your children have never tasted it.

Fried Zucchini

1. Let the children wash, peel, and cut the zucchini into $1/2$ in. (13 mm) thick rings.
2. Dip in seasoning salt and flour.
3. Using an electric skillet, fry the rings. Remove the cooked zucchini from the hot grease with cooking tongs. Place the rings on paper towels to drain. Serve the zucchini warm.

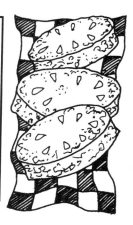

Zucchini Sticks and Dip

Zucchini is a great vegetable to dip.
1. Use plastic serrated knives to peel the zucchini and cut into sticks.
2. Dip in onion dip, sour cream, ranch dressing, mayonnaise, or any other favorite dip.

Stuffed Zucchini

1. Wash zucchini and cut off the stem. Using an apple corer, scoop out the pulp while taking care not to break the skin. One end should remain closed. Save the pulp.
2. To make the filling for each zucchini, mix 2 tbsp. (30 mL) pizza or spaghetti sauce and 2 tbsp. (30 mL) chopped zucchini pulp in a bowl. Stuff the mixture into the zucchini.
3. Layer the stuffed zucchini in a pan. Cover with stewed tomatoes or spaghetti sauce. Put a lid on the pan and cook over very low heat for 1 hour or until the zucchini is tender.

141

Sing the ABC Song

RHYME: Alphabet Song
A, B, C, D, E, F, G,
H, I, J, K, L, M, N, O, P,
Q, R, S, T, U, V, W, X, Y, and Z.
Now I know my ABCs.
Aren't you very proud of me?

Directions: Most children have heard "The Alphabet Song" sung to the tune of "Twinkle, Twinkle, Little Star." Practice singing the lyrics to make sure everyone can say the letters from start to finish. Then play a relay singing game.

The leader points to a child who sings "A." Then she points to another child who sings "B." See if the children can continue the rhythm and tune of the song as letters are sung by different children. The leader directs the alphabet choir with hand signals. This kind of singing in relay can be fun. When everyone knows the tune and the alphabet, try speeding up the song a bit. Do not put anyone on the spot. If a child does not know the letter, sing it for her so the song flows without interruption.

Alternative: Have the groups sing alternating letters. Example: Boys begin with "A." Girls chime in with "B," etc., or break it into lines as follows:

Group 1	A, B, C, D, E, F, G,
Group 2	H, I, J, K, L, M, N, O, P,
Group 1	Q, R, S,
Group 2	T, U, V,
Group 1	W, X,
Group 2	Y, and Z
All	Now I know my ABCs.
	Aren't you very proud of me?

Alphabet Exchange

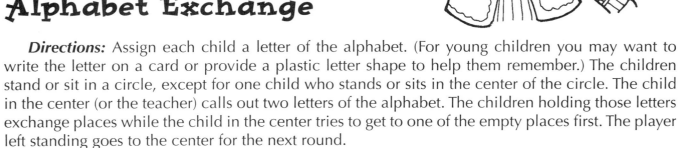

Directions: Assign each child a letter of the alphabet. (For young children you may want to write the letter on a card or provide a plastic letter shape to help them remember.) The children stand or sit in a circle, except for one child who stands or sits in the center of the circle. The child in the center (or the teacher) calls out two letters of the alphabet. The children holding those letters exchange places while the child in the center tries to get to one of the empty places first. The player left standing goes to the center for the next round.

142

Alphabet Word Hunt

Name

Directions: Look in books to find a word that begins with each letter. Copy each word next to the correct letter below.

A _____

B _____

C _____

D _____

E _____

F _____

G _____

H _____

I _____

J _____

K _____

L _____

M _____

N _____

O _____

P _____

Q _____

R _____

S _____

T _____

U _____

V _____

W _____

X _____

Y _____

Z _____

Zoo Search

Name _____

Directions: Somewhere in the zoo is an animal for each letter of the alphabet. Find the animals: alligator, bird, cat, dog, elephant, fish, goat, horse, iguana, jellyfish, kangaroo, llama, monkey, newt, ostrich, porcupine, quail, rhinoceros, snake, turtle, unicorn, vulture, walrus, xenopus (a toad), yak, and zebra. Next to each animal, print the first letter of its name. Color the picture.

Getting Ready: Reproduce two sets of cards (pages 145–147) onto card stock. Color and cut apart the cards. For durability, laminate them or cover each one with clear self-adhesive plastic.

Directions: This game can be played by two to four players. Shuffle and deal seven cards to each player. Place the remaining cards facedown in a pile. First player draws a card and looks to see if he has a matching pair of cards. If he does, he lays the pair down in front of him. If not, he discards one card from his hand. The next player can choose the card on top of the draw pile or take the last card that was discarded. There are two wild cards in the deck and they can be used with any animal to make a pair. If there are no more cards to select from, the discard pile is shuffled and placed facedown. The game continues until one player has collected four pairs and is declared the winner.

Zoo Animal Matchup

Aa alligator

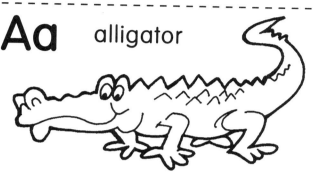

RHYME: "Z" Is a Zebra
"Z" is a zebra
That you've heard of before;
So here ends my rhyme
Till I find you some more.

Bb   bird

Cc

cat

Dd

dog

Ee

elephant

Ff

fish

Gg

goat

Hh horse

Ii iguana

Jj jellyfish

Kk kangaroo

Ll llama

Mm monkey

Nn newt

Oo ostrich

Pp porcupine

Qq quail

Rr robin

Ss seal

Tt turtle

Uu unicorn

Vv vulture

Ww wolf

Xx xenopus

Yy yak

Zz zebra

Wild Card

Learning ABC's Through Literature and Rhymes

My ABC Book

To make a fold-out ABC book, use the patterns on pages 148–151. You may want to have older children help you assemble the books ahead of time for the younger children.

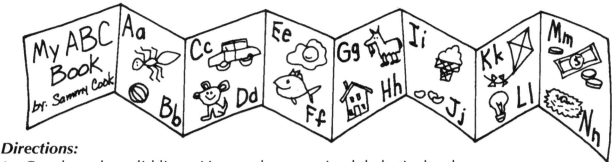

Directions:

1. Cut along the solid lines. Line up the pages in alphabetical order.
2. Overlap the sections and glue along the dotted edges at both ends of each page. Double check to make sure the pages are in alphabetical order before you glue them together to assemble the booklet. Let the glue dry.
3. Fold along the dotted line at the center of each page so that the book will fold up.
4. Draw and color a picture for each letter of the alphabet.
5. Draw a picture for the cover.
6. Print or find someone to print the word for each of the pictures in the book.

Cc

Ee

Overlap and glue.

Dd

Ff

Gg

Ii

Overlap and glue.

Hh

Jj

Learning ABC's Through Literature and Rhymes

Kk

Mm

Ll

Nn

Overlap and glue.

Oo

Qq

Pp

Rr

Overlap and glue.

Ss

Uu

Overlap and glue.

Tt

Vv

Ww

Yy

Overlap and glue.

Xx

Zz

They Swallowed the Alphabet!

Directions: Culminate the alphabet units by having the children learn the story *They Swallowed the Alphabet!* Reproduce the following verses for each child. Help the children staple the pages in alphabetical order and make covers for the books. Arrange for the children to perform the entire text for parents or another class.

They Swallowed the Alphabet!

A a A a A a A a A a A a

I know some children who swallowed some A's.
And I am amazed;
they swallowed those A's.
How very brave.

B b B b B b B b B b B b

I know some children who swallowed some B's,
They swallowed some B's
that bumped in their bellies
and bounced to their knees.
I know some children who swallowed some A's.
And I am amazed;
they swallowed those A's.
How very brave.

Cc Cc Cc Cc
cC Cc Cc Cc

I know some children who swallowed
some C's,
Not crackers or candy, just cups full of C's.
They swallowed some C's
and swallowed some B's
that bumped in their bellies
and bounced to their knees.
I know some children who swallowed some A's.
And I am amazed; they swallowed those A's.
How very brave.

Dd Dd Dd Dd
dd Dd Dd Dd

I know some children who swallowed
some D's,
They dunked them like
doughnuts and down went the D's.
They swallowed some C's
and swallowed some B's
that bumped in their bellies
and bounced to their knees.
I know some children who swallowed some A's.
And I am amazed; they swallowed those A's.
How very brave.

Ee Ee Ee Ee
ee Ee Ee Ee

I know some children who swallowed
some E's,
It wasn't easy to eat all those E's.
They swallowed some E's
and swallowed some D's.
They swallowed some C's
and swallowed some B's
that bumped in their bellies
and bounced to their knees.
I know some children who swallowed some A's.
And I am amazed; they swallowed those A's.
How very brave.

Ff Ff Ff Ff
ff Ff Ff Ff

I know some children who swallowed
some F's,
All of them feasted on fistfuls of F's.
They swallowed some F's, some E's and D's.
They swallowed some C's
and swallowed some B's
that bumped in their bellies
and bounced to their knees.
I know some children who swallowed some A's.
And I am amazed; they swallowed those A's.
How very brave.

Gg Gg G
g GGg G g

I know some children who swallowed
some G's.
They gleefully gobbled down gallons of G's.
They swallowed some F's, some E's and D's.
They swallowed some C's
and swallowed some B's
that bumped in their bellies
and bounced to their knees.
I know some children who swallowed some A's.
And I am amazed; they swallowed those A's.
How very brave.

Hh H h H
h h h H h

I know some children who swallowed
some H's.
They heaped them high and had some H's.
They swallowed some G's—F's, E's, and D's.
They swallowed some C's
and swallowed some B's
that bumped in their bellies
and bounced to their knees.
I know some children who swallowed some A's.
And I am amazed; they swallowed those A's.
How very brave.

I i I i I
i i I I i

I know some children who swallowed
some I's.
Sliding inside, I after I.
They swallowed some I's and H's heaped high.
They swallowed some G's—F's, E's, and D's.
They swallowed some C's
and swallowed some B's
that bumped in their bellies
and bounced to their knees.
I know some children who swallowed
some A's.
And I am amazed; they swallowed those A's.
How very brave.

J j J j J
j J J J j

I know some children who swallowed
some J's.
Not jelly or jam, just jars full of J's.
They swallowed some I's and H's heaped high.
They swallowed some G's—F's, E's, and D's.
They swallowed some C's
and swallowed some B's
that bumped in their bellies
and bounced to their knees.
I know some children who swallowed
some A's.
And I am amazed; they swallowed those A's.
How very brave.

K k K k K
k K K K k

I know some children who swallowed
some K's.
Kids get a kick out of swallowing K's.
They swallowed K's; they swallowed J's.
They swallowed some I's and H's heaped high.
They swallowed some G's—F's, E's, and D's.
They swallowed some C's
and swallowed some B's
that bumped in their bellies
and bounced to their knees.
I know some children who swallowed
some A's.
And I am amazed; they swallowed those A's.
How very brave.

L l L l L
l L L L l

I know some children who swallowed
some L's.
They licked their lips, then lapped up lots of L's.
They swallowed some L's and K's and J's.
They swallowed some I's and H's heaped high.
They swallowed some G's—F's, E's, and D's.
They swallowed some C's
and swallowed some B's
that bumped in their bellies
and bounced to their knees.
I know some children who swallowed
some A's.
And I am amazed; they swallowed those A's.
How very brave.

M m M M M
m M M M m

I know some children who swallowed
some M's.
They moaned as they munched up
mouthfuls of M's.
They swallowed some L's and K's and J's.
They swallowed some I's and H's heaped high.
They swallowed some G's—F's, E's, and D's.
They swallowed some C's
and swallowed some B's
that bumped in their bellies
and bounced to their knees.
I know some children who swallowed
some A's.
And I am amazed; they swallowed those A's.
How very brave.

N n N n N
n N N N n

I know some children who swallowed
some N's.
No napkins are needed when gnawing on N's.
They swallowed some N's
and swallowed some M's.
They swallowed some L's and K's and J's.
They swallowed some I's and H's heaped high.
They swallowed some G's—F's, E's, and D's.
They swallowed some C's
and swallowed some B's
that bumped in their bellies
and bounced to their knees.
I know some children who swallowed
some A's.
And I am amazed; they swallowed those A's.
How very brave.

I know some children who swallowed
some O's.
Oodles and oodles and oodles of O's.
They swallowed some N's
and swallowed some M's.
They swallowed some L's and K's and J's.
They swallowed some I's and H's heaped high.
They swallowed some G's—F's, E's, and D's.
They swallowed some C's
and swallowed some B's
that bumped in their bellies
and bounced to their knees.
I know some children who swallowed
some A's.
And I am amazed; they swallowed those A's.
How very brave.

I know some children who swallowed
some P's.
Pleased as punch, they packed in their P's.
They swallowed some P's and some O's, too.
They swallowed some N's
and swallowed some M's.
They swallowed some L's and K's and J's.
They swallowed some I's and H's heaped high.
They swallowed some G's—F's, E's, and D's.
They swallowed some C's
and swallowed some B's
that bumped in their bellies
and bounced to their knees.
I know some children who swallowed
some A's.
And I am amazed; they swallowed those A's.
How very brave.

I know some children who swallowed
some Q's.
They glued them to U's and swallowed the Q's.
They swallowed some P's and some O's, too.
They swallowed some N's
and swallowed some M's.
They swallowed some L's and K's and J's.
They swallowed some I's and H's heaped high.
They swallowed some G's—F's, E's, and D's.
They swallowed some C's
and swallowed some B's
that bumped in their bellies
and bounced to their knees.
I know some children who swallowed
some A's.
And I am amazed; they swallowed those A's.
How very brave.

I know some children who swallowed
some R's.
Not runny or rotten, just really ripe R's.
They swallowed some R's; they swallowed Q's.
They swallowed some P's and some O's, too.
They swallowed some N's
and swallowed some M's.
They swallowed some L's and K's and J's.
They swallowed some I's and H's heaped high.
They swallowed some G's—F's, E's, and D's.
They swallowed some C's
and swallowed some B's
that bumped in their bellies
and bounced to their knees.
I know some children who swallowed
some A's.
And I am amazed; they swallowed those A's.
How very brave

S s S s S s S s S s S S

I know some children who swallowed
some S's.
How sweet it is to swallow an S.
They swallowed some R's; they swallowed Q's.
They swallowed some P's and some O's, too.
They swallowed some N's
and swallowed some M's.
They swallowed some L's and K's and J's.
They swallowed some I's and H's heaped high.
They swallowed some G's—F's, E's, and D's.
They swallowed some C's
and swallowed some B's
that bumped in their bellies
and bounced to their knees.
I know some children who swallowed
some A's.
And I am amazed; they swallowed those A's.
How very brave.

T t T t T t T t T t T T

I know some children who swallowed
some T's.
They tickled their tongues with tiny, tart T's.
They swallowed some T's—S's, R's, and Q's.
They swallowed some P's and some O's, too.
They swallowed some N's
and swallowed some M's.
They swallowed some L's and K's and J's.
They swallowed some I's and H's heaped high.
They swallowed some G's—F's, E's, and D's.
They swallowed some C's
and swallowed some B's
that bumped in their bellies
and bounced to their knees.
I know some children who swallowed
some A's.
And I am amazed; they swallowed those A's.
How very brave

U u U u U u U u U u U U

I know some children who swallowed
some U's.
It simply is true, they swallowed some U's.
They swallowed some T's—S's, R's, and Q's.
They swallowed some P's and some O's, too.
They swallowed some N's
and swallowed some M's.
They swallowed some L's and K's and J's.
They swallowed some I's and H's heaped high.
They swallowed some G's—F's, E's, and D's.
They swallowed some C's
and swallowed some B's
that bumped in their bellies
and bounced to their knees.
I know some children who swallowed
some A's.
And I am amazed; they swallowed those A's.
How very brave.

I know some children who swallowed
some V's.
This is the verse where they swallowed
their V's.
They swallowed some V's
and swallowed some U's.
They swallowed some T's—S's, R's, and Q's.
They swallowed some P's
and some O's, too.
They swallowed some N's
and swallowed some M's.
They swallowed some L's and K's and J's.
They swallowed some I's and H's heaped high.
They swallowed some G's—F's, E's, and D's.
They swallowed some C's
and swallowed some B's
that bumped in their bellies
and bounced to their knees.
I know some children who swallowed
some A's.
And I am amazed; they swallowed those A's.
How very brave.

157
Learning ABC's Through Literature and Rhymes

W W W w

I know some children who swallowed
some W's.
Without any trouble, they swallowed W's.
They swallowed some V's
and swallowed some U's.
They swallowed some T's—S's, R's, and Q's.
They swallowed some P's and some O's, too.
They swallowed some N's
and swallowed some M's.
They swallowed some L's and K's and J's.
They swallowed some I's and H's heaped high.
They swallowed some G's—F's, E's, and D's.
They swallowed some C's
and swallowed some B's
that bumped in their bellies
and bounced to their knees.
I know some children who swallowed
some A's.
And I am amazed; they swallowed those A's.
How very brave.

I know some children who swallowed
some X's.
You wouldn't expect them to pass up
those X's.
They swallowed some W's.
They swallowed some V's
and swallowed some U's.
They swallowed some T's—S's, R's, and Q's.
They swallowed some P's and some O's, too.
They swallowed some N's
and swallowed some M's.
They swallowed some L's and K's and J's.
They swallowed some I's and H's heaped high.
They swallowed some G's—F's, E's, and D's.
They swallowed some C's
and swallowed some B's
that bumped in their bellies
and bounced to their knees.
I know some children who swallowed
some A's.
And I am amazed; they swallowed those A's.
How very brave.

I know some children who swallowed
some Y's.
Yes, it was yummy to swallow those Y's.
They swallowed some X's and W's.
They swallowed some V's
and swallowed some U's.
They swallowed some T's—S's, R's, and Q's.
They swallowed some P's and some O's, too.
They swallowed some N's
and swallowed some M's.
They swallowed some L's and K's and J's.
They swallowed some I's and H's heaped high.
They swallowed some G's—F's, E's, and D's.
They swallowed some C's
and swallowed some B's
that bumped in their bellies
and bounced to their knees.
I know some children who swallowed
some A's.
And I am amazed; they swallowed those A's.
How very brave.

I know some children who
swallowed some Z's.
They now read with ease.

The End!